Learning to Play, Playing to Learn

From: Cheryl Farb Cash Elem.

Learning to Play, Playing to Learn

GAMES AND ACTIVITIES TO TEACH SHARING, CARING, AND COOPERATION

by Charlie Steffens *and* Spencer Gorin

illustrations by Spencer Gorin
with a foreword by Dennis Embry, PeaceBuilders

1-800-742-0708
Website: www.joyinlearning.com

We encourage participants to use their own good judgment when monitoring their well-being and activity levels. Creative Spirit assumes no liability for injuries.

Learning to Play, Playing to Learn
by Charlie Steffens and Spencer Gorin
First Edition 1997, Second Edition 2004

Library of Congress Cataloging-in-Publication Data

Steffens, Charlie.
Learning to play, playing to learn / by Charlie Steffens and Spencer Gorin; illustrations by Spencer Gorin; with a foreword by Dennis Embry.
p. cm.
Includes bibliographical references and index.
ISBN 0-9747533-1-9
1. Play. 2. Games. 3. Creative activities and seat work. 4. Socialization. 5. Play therapy. I. Gorin, Spencer. II. Title.
LB1137.S76 1997
155.4'18—dc21 97-38131

Requests for such permissions should be addressed to:
Creative Spirit
2545 West Rapallo Way
Tucson, AZ 85741
1-800-742-0708

Publishing Consultant: Linda F. Radke, Five Star Publications, Inc.
Chandler, Arizona, www.FiveStarPublications.com
Design: Kate Mueller, Electric Dragon Productions & Rich Foster, Rich Designs
Cover Photo: SuperStock Inc.

Manufactured in the United States of America
10 9 8 7 6 5 4 3 2

Contents

Acknowledgments

We at Creative Spirit would like to acknowledge all the playful and creative spirit-masters who have been inspiration for our endeavors. Special thanks are directed toward the wizards at the New Games and Playfair foundations, PeaceBuilders, Ann Herbert, and Terry Orlick. This book is intended to promote healthy socialization through play and humor. Our Healthy Play Is a Solution/Learning to Play program is designed to educate people so everyone may achieve all the meaningful benefits associated with play.

The authors gratefully acknowledge the following sources for their contribution to this book:

Giants, elves, and wizards; blob; and the five Cs are adapted from *New Games & More New Games* © 1981 by Andrew Fluegelman. Reproduced for Creative Spirit by permission of Bantam Doubleday Dell Publishing Group, Inc. (1540 Broadway, New York, New York 10036). Further reproduction is prohibited.

Rolling logs, cooperative musical chairs, and dragons dodgeball are adapted from the first and second *Cooperative Sports &*

Foreword

"Let's play," invites Jimmy.

"But we can't, because the game machine is broken on the TV and it's raining," groans Ray.

"We can create something fun," Jimmy replies.

As a wise person sitting on the sidelines, you notice this interaction. You've been asked to make a prediction about which child is going to do well in life. So, you stick around and watch some more, because you want to make a sound judgment. Here is what you see:

Jimmy recruits the whole class to play. Ray says, "Don't ask the new kids to play, they're dorks."

Jimmy announces, "We could play basketball or we could play, are you a PeaceBuilder? Which game would help the new kids learn everybody's names?" Ray complains, "Argh . . . that's so lame."

All the kids join in to play are you a PeaceBuilder?—which is a game somewhat like musical chairs, except that no chairs get removed. There is much laughing, turn taking, and learning of names and interests that students share. Ray tries to hog the middle, and he squabbles about getting the chairs first. Sometimes, Ray calls the other kids names or shoves them. Jimmy has a constant smile on his face, and he makes suggestions to change the pace of the game or its focus. Other children praise him for his ideas.

Which young person is more likely to succeed in the world? Jimmy or Ray? Which one is more likely to receive a great deal of positive teacher attention? Which one is more likely to be liked by other kids? Which one is more likely to have positive relationships with his family and siblings? Which one is less likely to get into trouble with the law or abuse drugs? Jimmy.

Jimmy used to be like Ray. He didn't know how to play. He didn't know how to have fun. He had to learn both. He got Creative Spirit. Jimmy isn't his real name, yet I know many kids like him who have learned to play cooperatively and compassionately. It helped them become successful with peers and adults.

Here is the simple truth. What children play, they become as adults. Two simple twenty-minute observations of children's behavior during recess in the fifth grade can help predict juvenile delinquency five years later. During play, children develop skills that help them in life, and they learn how to inhibit other actions. Here are some of the skills that can be mastered in play.

Social competencies to increase:

- ✓ Sharing laughter with peers
- ✓ Compromising with peers when a situation calls for it
- ✓ Responding to teasing or name calling by ignoring, changing the subject, or some other constructive means
- ✓ Accepting constructive criticism from peers without becoming angry
- ✓ Talking with peers appropriately for extended periods of time
- ✓ Initiating conversations with peers in informal situations
- ✓ Appropriately coping with aggression from others (e.g., trying to avoid a fight, walking away)

- ✓ Interacting with a number of different peers
- ✓ Accepting not getting one's own way
- ✓ Attending to assigned tasks

Behaviors to decrease or inhibit:

- ✓ Excessive arguing
- ✓ Bragging or boasting
- ✓ Cruelty, bullying
- ✓ Demanding a lot of attention
- ✓ Destroying property that belongs to others
- ✓ Disobeying people in positions of responsibility
- ✓ Disturbing other people
- ✓ Getting jealous easily
- ✓ Getting in fights
- ✓ Physically attacking people
- ✓ Showing off or clowning around
- ✓ Explosiveness and unpredictability
- ✓ Insisting that demands be met immediately
- ✓ Stubbornness, sullenness, irritability
- ✓ Talking too much
- ✓ Teasing a lot
- ✓ Threatening people
- ✓ Talking unusually loudly

What kind of play teaches these skills best? Unstructured hanging out? Highly competitive games? Or structured, cooperative games and activities? The answer is quite clear: structured, organized, cooperative games. The effects are staggering when examined scientifically. Rates of aggression will drop by 50 percent or more on the playground, just by having organized, cooperative games. Cooperative games can reduce racism on the playground. Cooperative games also reduce negative behavior toward developmentally delayed children. Cooperative games may also allow socially rejected students a chance to build confidence gradually. They may then join in high-status rough-and-tumble games without losing control and further status.

Cooperative games *alone* are not a cure for behavior problems. One must combine the games with good behavior-management strategies, such as showing positive emotions instead of hostility and creating both group rewards for cooperation and clear-cut consequences for negative behavior. Such consequences are most effective if they are short, clearly defined time-outs or "sit-and watches," in which the child sees other kids having lots of fun and the play environment is safe physically, emotionally, and socially. Socratic-style questions from supervising adults help students think through what they have done and what they might do to make their lives more fun and filled with friends and to feel better about themselves. Is there anything that combines all these wise principles?

The information found in *Learning to Play, Playing to Learn* and the Healthy Play Is a Solution program meets the criteria of what enhances the development of children. That is why PeaceBuilders enlisted Creative Spirit founders Charlie Steffens and Spencer Gorin as collaborators in the design of a universal playground intervention for inclusion in a long-term study with the U.S. Centers for Disease Control and Prevention on scientifically valid ways to reduce youth violence. As a child psychologist with a good deal of study in anthropology, I was attracted to the Creative Spirit work. Structuring children's play made much more sense to me practically and scientifically than creating miniature versions of our legal and mental-health system on the playground.

How big is the aggression problem on a playground? One study shows the rates are about 700 acts per hour. Very high-risk schools or groups may have higher and much more serious rates of aggression. In our first study, published in the *American Journal of Preventive Medicine,* 12 percent of our sample of third through fifth graders reported having been threatened with a knife or gun on campus in the past week. What are the implications of 700 acts of aggression per hour? If each one of those acts went to some kind of conflict mediation for one-minute, the school would have about ten hours of conflict mediation time. Of course that doesn't happen—only a few children go through some sort of mediation process.

The potential long-term danger for both nonaggressive and aggressive children may be greater now. Highly aggressive kids may become adept at bullying behavior and learn how to evade getting caught. Children who have been traumatized at home or in the neighborhood learn that adults and society cannot protect them from being retraumatized by violence, and that lesson severely harms future child development. All this begins to look a bit more like *Lord of the Flies.* Sending the traumatized or aggressive children to see a counselor at this point makes almost no sense and is certainly not likely to achieve any scientifically valid or practical results.

In my own scientific and practical work in hundreds of schools, I have seen the ideas and lessons of Spencer Gorin and Charlie Steffens work. Healthy play is a solution! How do I know this? Well, first I see and feel it from being with the children and teachers. Second, I see it in our longitudinal data being collected with the Centers for Disease Control. One of our studies just being published shows that children in our research schools are healthier and freer from both intentional and unintentional injuries. This makes sense from what we now know from the scientific study of health and immunology. Our direct observational data across our research schools also shows less aggression on the playground, and the students report less aggression to and from their peers.

The kind of strategies proposed by this book does make sense, both practically and scientifically. The strategies in this book also make cents. If aggression is reduced on the playground and in classrooms, homes, and neighborhoods, there will be fewer placements in special education and fewer injuries and lawsuits.

Human beings are most certainly genetically programmed to *copy* play they see other children or adults do. If children see adults or other children playing aggressively or just hanging out, that is what they will do. If children see cooperative play, they will copy that. Such a skill makes obvious, profound adaptive sense. This process of imitation of play is so fundamental to ethnology and human psychology, it has almost become invisible—with results that may completely alter the future of humanity if present trends continue.

Children and adults no longer know how to play. They know how to be entertained. Children and the adults who love and care for them now have to learn how to play in a way that restores the spirit, hope, and fun. This book is a book of wisdom. It is a book that helps return play to its two must important purposes: fun and people. This book teaches us how to put the fun and people back into play. If I were to require two books for every new teacher, they would be Harry Wong's *The First Day of School* and Spencer Gorin and Charlie Steffens's *Learning to Play, Playing to Learn.* Our children must learn to read, write, and add. Our children must also learn to live wisely in compassion and joy. Without other people, learning is not likely. Without fun, life is without joy. *Learning to Play, Playing to Learn* helps children learn and experience joy.

Dennis D. Embry, Ph.D.
Cofounder of PeaceBuilders

How to Use This Book

The basic premise of *Learning to Play, Playing to Learn,* demonstrated in our Healthy Play Is a Solution program, is that therapeutic play can provide a solution to contemporary socialization problems. This text has a school-related focus with a target audience of teachers, parents, church and synagogue groups, parks and recreation staffs, and community leaders.

All the materials in this book are presented in a practical and logical order. This logical progression of activities guarantees greater success upon implementation. We encourage you to understand and use the game types ("creative," "compassionate," and "soft aggression" play) in succession as they are presented. But you do not have to follow each game in the order that it is presented. We want you, as a reader, to feel free to move at your most comfortable pace. Discover your own readiness. Come to know the readiness of your own group. To implement the program and to achieve the desired behaviors, you must first assess your group's needs.

Each game is described and followed by a "Gift of the Game" section. This may be a vignette based on what we have observed or a touching story told by a parent or teacher. It may also indicate which behaviors can be nurtured by playing the activity and/or other benefits that might not be immediately apparent. At the end of the book, you will find more helpful tips to maximize the benefits of play.

Finally, please note that this book has two authors. We want to celebrate both our partnership and the individuality that went into creating *Learning to Play, Playing to Learn.* Our writing styles may reflect this. Sometimes one or the other of us will be addressing the reader directly with personal experiences or feelings. For the most part, however, we will be addressing you jointly. As a reader, you should imagine that we, both Charlie and Spencer, are there with you as we address concerns and questions that you may have. We want you to be able to celebrate the group as well as the individuals that you will be working and playing with.

Introduction

This book is about discovering the freedom to be creative, innovative, and humorous. It is about giving permission to take risks and succeed in life, both at work and at play. It is about recapturing the attributes that make us good neighbors, workers, bosses, parents, teachers, and friends. And it is about passing those wonderfully infectious values to those who are in and around our hearts. This book is about rediscovering ourselves and others through the most basic and fun way possible: healthy play.

I, Spencer, was less than seven when I began truly to learn about myself. By the time I was a teenager, I had learned all that I could bear to know. Even though I knew that I was basically okay, an inner voice kept telling me that I was never good enough, fast enough, smart enough, or popular enough and certainly not tough enough. And, no, I didn't get those messages from my parents. They were both adoring and nurturing parents. I got many of those negative messages every day from my friends and peers at school, in gym, on the playgrounds, and in the backyards of my neighborhood.

I was just having fun, playing, doing kids' work. But the taunts, teasing, and bullying made playtime so unbearable that I withdrew into a world of drawing, playing music, and other enjoyable but ultimately isolating activities. I would never be good enough around my peers, and I certainly could not feel safe around many of them. I felt shame when I needed to feel trust. I got criticism when I needed compliments, so I quit taking risks and stopped socializing when I should have been reaching out. I wasn't alone in experiencing these self-defeating feelings and behaviors. As I grew to adulthood, others shared their stories about their difficult and often humiliating play experiences. The stories were so familiar.

Where were the adults to help nurture us, to teach us to "play fair" and "play nice"? They usually weren't there in the backyards, on the playgrounds, the streets—the kids' turf. Sometimes there was a momentary reprieve at school when a teacher just happened to catch one of those students teasing or hurting us. Adults told us, "It's not that you win, it's how you play the game that counts," but very few of us experienced play that way. The games we played, especially the organized sports taught to us by the adults, were full of hard lessons about human nature: Play to win by defeating others; might is right; someone has to lose; you can't change the rules; you're with the in crowd as long as you win; and there is no room for failure. Speed, strength, and cunning are the attributes we worship.

Along the way, we integrated these values and carried them into adulthood. Now we would rather watch television than go dancing. We lock our doors at night because we don't trust others. We take no chances at work because there is no room for failure. We're overweight because we've lost personal kinetic excitement. We can't make or accept compliments because we've become masters of the put-down. It seems that someone is always better, and success is for others. We're alone because we don't know how to share. Our children fight and hurt each other.

We learn many hurtful and helpful behaviors as children through our play experiences. We learn about "relatedness" and socialization through our play. The reason so few adults and many children are no longer playful is that we've had the play beaten out of us. Play is no longer seen or experienced as being fun, and as a culture, we see little value in play or fun.

Most adult's and children's sports and game activities don't protect our sense of self-esteem or self-worth. Too few people play fair anymore, and the majority of us end up feeling like losers. That is why we've stopped playing, and that is why as a culture we have stopped winning in the arenas of relationships, marriage, industry, and education. How can we love our spouses when we haven't learned to share, care, or compromise? How can we work together when we can't cooperate with our coworkers? And how can we learn in our schools when we fear for our self-concept, safety, even our lives?

We can't.

Or rather, we can't if we continue on this fearful and hurtful path.

The good news is that we can meet all our needs when we choose to change our attitudes and values about how we play and work with each other. As we change our ways of thinking, we change our behaviors, and our interactions with others become more successful and intimate. Our process awakens our sense of joy and pleasure. At school, we can get on with learning because we are not distracted by ridicule and threats. At the office, we can get on with business because we have discovered how to maximize cooperation and teamwork. And at home, we can return to love because we have learned how to communicate and nurture.

"But wait," you're thinking. "Weren't you just talking about play? I don't get the connection." The connection has been there all along—it's just been a negative one. You've brought all those negative lessons that you learned in your play into your life, your work, your home.

In 1992, Charlie and I cofounded Creative Spirit. Creative Spirit became dedicated to the notion that creativity, humor, and play are the foundations of improved personal and professional performance. For businesses, we created a program called the Professional Applications of Play on Productivity. Our other venture, Healthy Play Is a Solution, has been delivered to thousands of organizations, groups, and individuals, who live and work in the trenches with our children and teenagers, a successful, effective, and fun program that promotes and manages positive social behaviors. The Healthy Play program evolved from the many years that we had successfully utilized play activities to manage the most challenging children, families, and adults in both mental health and educational settings. We found that healthy play was a simple and eloquent solution to many problems facing our youth. Through play we were able to manage aggressive behaviors, foster cooperation, and nurture positive conduct. Learning to play is a healthy solution. This is why the book has been titled *Learning to Play, Playing to Learn.*

Learning to Play, Playing to Learn is dedicated to reintroducing healthy socialization through play and humor. The many benefits of healthy playfulness and humor are open to all. It is important that we as individuals and as a society implement what is idealistic, realistic, and practical about play.

Successful learning is accomplished by playing. This concept must be acknowledged and stressed. Play is intended to be the safe arena where we can practice and fail, and practice and practice some more so that self-improvement is constantly achieved. Play is not just a set of time-consuming activities that we do until we grow up and become workers. It is an essential mechanism that allows us to learn how to become good parents, friends, workers, and, ultimately, creative, patient, caring, and honest human beings. Whether you are a parent, a teacher, a manager, a nurse, a doctor, a man, a woman, a child, you will find creativity, humor, and play essential methods of improving personal and professional performance.

Throughout this book, you will find more than sixty unique and entertaining activities. Along with a description of each activity, we have often included a concrete benefit ("The Gift of the

Game") that comes from participating in that activity, beyond the P, F & G (pure fun and giggles) factor. In some instances, we'll describe a playground setting. Other times, it may be a family or classroom setting. Yet each activity can be easily altered, so the benefits are available to any participants in any setting.

While reading this book, you will be given the knowledge and the tools to create a safe and nurturing experience. If you focus on the needs of your participants first and foremost, the magic of individual and collective experiences will open up harmonious, socially satisfying, and productive forces. We would like to invite you to join with us in discovering how many ways healthy play is a solution to contemporary challenges confronting our youth. We invite you to open your heart, mind, and body as you discover the joys of learning to play and playing to learn.

If you have any questions or want more information regarding this book or Healthy Play resources, you can contact the authors, toll-free, at 1-800-742-0708, or write to us care of Creative Spirit, 6062 East Beverly, Tucson, Arizona 85711.

Never stop laughing! Never stop playing!

About Play

In the beginning—well, soon after, anyway—there was play.

Every culture has developed and used play as a means to teach children the necessary skills of living. Playing is not a way for children to waste time until they finally grow up and get a job. It is the *natural way* for children to learn. Through play, children can practice over and over and over the behaviors and tasks necessary to become adults. This process is essential in all grade levels of education.

Until about seventy-five years ago, it was easy to correlate the usefulness of play activities with becoming a successful adult. Play activities centered around food gathering, hunting, animal husbandry, clothes making, and mock parenting. Recently, as we have become more urbanized, the development of play has been focused on two areas: entertainment and competition. These two concepts of play have been somewhat useful in helping humanity cope with living in compact cities. However, far too frequently, entertainment and competition have become overused extremes that no longer represent the true meaning of play and its educational potential.

Millions of dollars have been spent on play research, and volumes of reports have been written documenting the values of play. It is not our goal to add any more academic rhetoric that intellectualizes, rationalizes, or microanalyzes play dynamics. These excesses have overcomplicated play issues and created a perception that only those with Ph.D.'s can use the play process beneficially. Creative Spirit believes it's time to empower everyone to just start playing in a healthy manner.

About the Healthy Solution

Promote Healthy Social Skills

We named our program Healthy Play Is a Solution because play is *one* of the solutions to what ails our troubled times. The program, and this book, are designed to allow children to learn and develop healthy, positive social skills while playing. This is the real goal: healthy social skills. When play is monitored by caring elders (such as parents, teachers, and youth leaders), wonderful gifts will be discovered.

Manage Aggressive Behaviors

You can use healthy play to reduce and manage aggressive behaviors in your class and at home. When taught by teachers during class time, healthy-play behaviors transfer to free-play settings and throughout the entire school community. That's why one principal at a school said after Healthy Play activities began, "It has been two and a half months since I've had a recess playground referral of a student for problem behaviors in my office." A safe school environment becomes the foundation where learning will occur.

Increase Self-Esteem

Every child can be nurtured to develop a positive self-concept. It isn't enough to talk or read about having good self-esteem. Children are far too concrete in their thinking to learn that way. Self-esteem is something that develops from things you do. *Learning to Play* ideals can make good things happen for everyone.

Develop Social Relatedness

Play is where you really practice how to get along with others and to make friends. Regardless of what your future GPA or SAT scores are, it is essential to learn the skills that allow you to relate socially to others. Developing successful social-relatedness skills is a fundamental part of every child's education.

Maximize Participation

The Creative Spirit approach gets every person involved. Once you broaden your play focus beyond "who's best," all students will be willing to try to be their own bests. All kids really want to play, but only when it's safe and when they know they can't be physically or emotionally hurt.

Promote Positive Life Values

Healthy play promotes positive life values. Children will practice caring, sharing, and being compassionate and honest. More important, healthy play activities become the arena where children take personal responsibility for their actions. A key to this program is holding every student accountable for the things he or she does. What you really want to do is to reinforce the things they are doing very, very well. You'll find that healthy play encourages such comments as "Gee, that's a great job," or "Thanks for taking care of me." Peers and elders alike will learn to praise each person's accomplishments during a game. Likewise, it is everyone's caring responsibility to critique areas where a child's behavior needs improvement and where additional learning needs to occur. These issues can be safely addressed during Healthy Play activities.

Increase Emotional and Physical Health

Playing daily is good for students' physical and emotional health. Kids don't have six-hour attention spans. They really don't. Really! Once you get past the limited concept that play is just entertainment, you can start to use play as a healthy solution to all sorts of daily classroom problems.

When students just can't stay in their seats any longer, get them out of their seats. They have already stopped learning. You've stopped teaching. The situation has become an endless battle for control between you and the students. When play becomes a time for teaching social values, games become a valuable part of the curriculum. You're not just wasting time. Brief exercise and laughter will release natural body chemicals that will relax and stimulate more productive student behaviors. Developing a healthy heart, lungs, and muscles are not bad secondary benefits.

Develop a Positive Peer Culture

The last but certainly not the least of our key components is to develop a positive peer culture. We're going to use peer pressure as a tool for teaching desirable social behavior. We think of the negative aspects of peer pressure so often that we overlook positive aspects. We get lost in the fact that peer pressure is often why kids do drugs or join gangs. Peer pressure is also why we all brush our teeth, comb our hair, take a shower, stop at red lights, go at green lights, and create laws. As you will see, Healthy Play concepts reinforce and empower those students who demonstrate or are mastering positive values. Those children will receive lots of attention and will ultimately be in control of the class. The message that you and the positive peer culture will say is, "If you want to play in our class, this positive way of playing is how it will have to be done." Because the class will want to play, they will practice how to do it right. What the students learn and the culture they create will transfer to every aspect of the entire school day.

Philosophy

To utilize play therapeutically, you need to focus on two essential philosophical principles and two valuable rules.

Philosophical principles:

1. We play to have fun.
2. People are the most important part of all games.

Let's start at the beginning. First, we must unload the common assumption that children are the experts on play simply because they are children. If this were true, our playgrounds, schools, and neighborhoods would not be battlefields, and you wouldn't need to read this book. Children are *not* the experts on play. They have unlearned the ability to play enjoyably with each other. They have unfortunately forgotten or haven't been taught how to explore, imagine, and create. Their entertainment and play are created by others, and often children are isolated at the end of a computer joystick or keyboard. As responsible elders, we must recreate an environment where children can rediscover the value of being fully actualized human beings.

Creating a Healthy Play Program for Your Setting

Let us imagine that we are setting up the program in your classroom or with any group of children. (From here on, any reference to a classroom can be interpreted to mean any group of children or teenagers in any setting.) We must help children identify their own set of values and feelings that playing evokes. When children identify these values on their own, they are more likely to buy into the program. They are more likely to accept their own and their peers' ideas rather than being spoon-fed an adult's suggestions, especially as they get older. However, once they identify their values and feelings, we elders must be responsible for holding them accountable to those values.

The Healthy Play program starts with the creation of two posters on paper that reflect these "soon to be discovered" values. Each group of children must create their classroom's own play commandments. The posters become concrete tools based on two very important questions, which must be identified in all classroom settings.

Poster 1: Why Do We Play?

Using a big piece of butcher-block paper, at the top write the question Why do we play? In the middle of the paper, draw a big, empty circle with a number one near the edge of it.

The following script is a suggested way to present the creation of the posters to your class. It will foster a sense of playfulness right from the beginning:

TEACHER: We are going to create two posters from the answers to two very important questions that I'm going to ask. Now, the first question I'm going to ask is "Why do we play?" But I need to let everybody here know that we are going to answer this

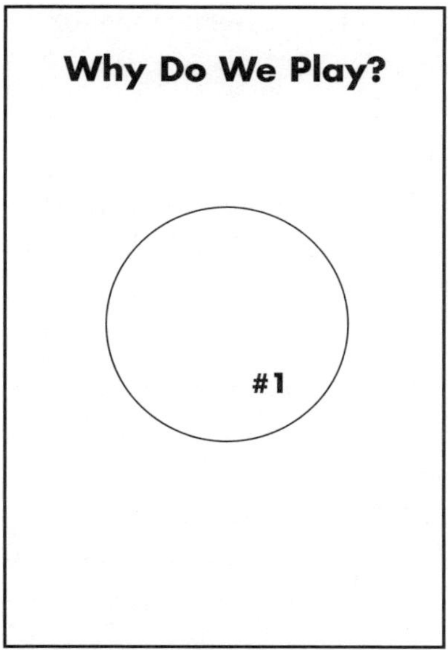

question as if we were on a TV game show. On our TV game show there is a number-one answer. I want to see it right here. [*Point to the circle with the number one in it.*] In addition to the number-one answer, there are going to be 101 other really great answers. All really important and great answers will be placed on our posters. And I'm going to choose *only* people who are being good listeners with their hands raised to answer this question. So, the first question I have is "Why do we play?" If you think you know the answer, raise your hand. All right, Molly, why do you play?

MOLLY: It's fun!

TEACHER: It is fun. Molly got the number-one answer. I need to let Molly know that if she were on an actual game show, she would have won the trip to Disneyland, the red convertible car, and the washer-dryer combination set. But since she's here at our elementary school, let's give her a big, loud round of applause. That *is* the number one answer. We play to have fun! Raise your hand if you also play to have fun. [*The kids raise their hands.*] It looks like almost everybody here plays to have fun! Who has another reason why we play? Why else would you play? Saul?

SAUL: Exercise.

TEACHER: Exercise. Great answer. Exercise builds strong muscles and good cardiovascular systems. Why else would we play?"

KATHY: To learn.

TEACHER: Exactly. Playing becomes a fantastic way to learn new things. And today we're going to learn new things. Cheryl, why do you play?

CHERYL: To make friends.

TEACHER: To make friends. That's a very important answer. [*When kids give the answer "to make friends," we generally stop the questioning for a moment and ask the children to raise their hands if they like to make friends. Everybody wants to make friends, and most students will raise their hands. Then we verbally and visually reinforce this for the students, saying, "If you want to make friends in this class, probably a great way to do it is to play with your friends. And seeing all the hands raised, many friendships can be found in our class." Adults know in an abstract way that the easiest cure for a sense of alienation is friendship, but children don't begin to experience the world abstractly until they are teenagers, so we must reinforce basic knowledge concretely and linearly. This is also how we start to develop a positive peer culture in each class.*]

TEACHER: Why else do we play? Amber?

AMBER: To relieve stress.

TEACHER: You're right. Play is a great way to relieve stress. Why else do we play?

JESSE: To create. To pretend

TEACHER: Oh, great answer. Why else?

MALIA: To share.

TEACHER: Excellent answer! Super answer.

ERNESTO: I play so I won't be bored. [*Boredom is a big issue for children and teenagers. Kids have a hard time finding things to do with themselves and with each other. Much of their entertainment is prepackaged for them. They need to learn how to entertain themselves.*]

TEACHER: Fantastic answer, Ernesto. I think being bored is totally boring. Who here also plays so that they won't be bored? Raise your hand.

While working on the same poster, ask the children about their feelings regarding play.

TEACHER: How do we like to feel when we are playing? Lucy, how do you like to feel?

LUCY: I like to feel happy.

TEACHER: Great answer. How else do we like to feel, Mike?

MIKE: Like a winner.

TEACHER: We all like to feel like we're winners. Raise your hand if you like to feel like you're a winner. Most of our sports and games are designed for one person to feel like that winner. But we are going to play games where everyone can feel like a winner because that's how we all want to feel, like winners. How else do we like to feel?

JANET: We want to be relaxed.

TEACHER: Ah, we want to be relaxed. There's a nice kind of exhaustion that sometimes comes from playing, from having a good time with ourselves and each other.

EDGAR: I want to feel included.

TEACHER: Me, too, Edgar. No one likes to be left out.

We know that children respond to buzzwords, so we invented one to help facilitate their buy-in to the program. Tell them of a feeling that you have when you play, and say you would like to include it on their poster. Tell them that when you play you like to feel *grex*. Write G-R-E-X on the poster and then look around to see the puzzled looks on their faces as they ponder what it could mean. Explain that the *gr* stands for the word *great,* and the *ex* stands for the word *excellent*. When you play, you like to feel both great and excellent, therefore you like to feel *grex.* Ask them to raise their right hands if they too want to feel great. They will respond quickly to your enthusiasm. Tell them to raise their left hands if they want to feel excellent. Their other hands will briskly go up. Their next instructions are to wave both hands in the air if they want to feel grex. It's at this point that I tell everyone that we are now applauding in American Sign Language. (Gee, we're learning something new already.) You now have the power of this playful buzzword at your disposal. It has facilitated laughter, smiles, and easy buy-in with children everywhere. Pretty grex, eh? The number of answers for your posters that you elicit from class to class may vary, but most primary classes can come up with about eight, while intermediates can call out up to fifteen. We've done literally thousands of classrooms, and the above-mentioned values are the ones we universally hear. It is now time to review the answers.

TEACHER: I think we've got enough great answers here. In this class, these are the reasons that we've identified as to why we play. We play to get exercise, to feel relaxed, so we won't be bored. We're going to learn when we play. We're going to play to create and pretend, to feel included, to feel happy and grex, to relieve our stress, to share, to feel like winners, and to be with our friends. But the number-one reason we play is to have what?

KIDS: Fun!

TEACHER: All right, you got the number-one answer. Okay, so once again, we play to have what?

KIDS: Fun!

Congratulations. You are one quarter of the way there, because this is the first philosophical tool and underlying principle for using play therapeutically. We play to have fun. Remind your children frequently that at their school the number-one reason they play is to have fun. This becomes the goal they must achieve when

they play. In fact, make "We play to have fun" your school's first mantra. If we can keep this simple underlying philosophy in mind, then all the other identified values gleaned from children regarding play and listed on our poster become available to us. Through play we learn rules, cooperation, responsibility, and much more. And, through the Healthy Play principles, children will learn healthy socialization and develop a greater chance of success in their lives.

Additionally, point out to the children that they didn't put such answers as playing to tease, humiliate, or hurt each other on their poster. Compliment them on the positive values they chose. Reiterate that they didn't put on the poster things that would prevent play from being fun, like teasing or hurting others.

TEACHER: These all are excellent reasons why we play. This is important because we are *all* going to be responsible for upholding and following through with these values. I don't see being sad, putting down, hurting, or humiliating anybody here on our poster. We were smart to leave them off. That is really important because those of us who can't follow through with these values will be asked not to participate. So what do you want to do, tease someone or have fun?

KIDS: Have fun!

TEACHER: Do you want to hurt others or have fun?

KIDS: Have fun!

Poster 2: What Is the Most Important Part of any Game?

The second essential part of our philosophy is to answer the question "What is the most important part of every game?" It doesn't matter if the game is jump rope, basketball, or hockey. It doesn't matter if it's chess, checkers, or duck, duck, goose. No matter what the game is, what is the single most important part of the game?

The answer to this question is the heart of Creative Spirit's Healthy Play Is a Solution program. Unlike the question "Why do we play?" (where "fun" was the obvious response), this second philosophical point has proven much more elusive for both adults and children. On discovering the answer, you will be able to see clearly why healthy play is such a valuable part of every school's daily curriculum.

To create the second poster, put another piece of paper on the wall with the second question written on top. Just like the first poster, have a big circle with a number one placed inside it, so the key response will be highlighted once it has been given. Now begin to solicit answers from your class.

In general, your students will give the following answers. "The most important part of the game is *winning, taking turns, teamwork, safety, being a good sport, cooperating, rules, playing fair,* or *no cheating*." Again, when you receive critical responses like "playing fair," briefly process this concept with the class and begin to solidify your system of positive peer pressure.

TEACHER: Who in this class likes it when we play fair during games? [*The majority of students will raise their hands.*] Who likes it when someone cheats or is dishonest? [*You may have some hands go up.*] Is it fun when there is cheating when we play?

CLASS: No! [*This will be the majority class answer. Here again, you are concretely helping your students identify a social skill they need to practice:* honesty. *During our class presentations, we like to ask for a show of hands for who doesn't think cheating is fun, and then ask the following.*]

TEACHER: With whom are you more likely to make friends: students who play fair or those who cheat? From now on, only those students who play fair will actively be involved in the game. We will give brief time-outs to students who are needing to learn how to play fairly. By watching, they can see how to have more success making friends. [*You have just put all the children with positive values in charge of the game.*]

Back to our question:

TEACHER: What is the most important part of every game? You have yet to discover the number-one answer. However, I do like all of your other answers, which indicate other important factors in all games. I agree, it is important to have fun, show respect, feel challenged, get better, participate, be responsible, have and take care of the equipment.

In many classes, students will readily supply their "no" list: no fighting, no kicking, no pushing, no hitting, no bad words. We like to list these responses because the children are used to hearing the values expressed this way. They just need the elders to help them follow through correctly when they are playing.

By now you must be wondering what is the most important part of every game? Here's a hint: You can't play any games without this part. Ahhh! The light goes on. *People* are the most important part of every game. Make a big deal of this. Switch the lights on and off several times, whistle, cheer, clap, and boldly write "people" in your number-one circle on your poster.

It is amazing that something as obvious as this essential philosophical point about healthy play is so overlooked. Ask your students:

- ✓ Are there any games without people?
- ✓ Do jump ropes jump by themselves?
- ✓ Do basketballs roll out of the classroom and start scoring by themselves?
- ✓ Do the puzzles glide off the shelves and put themselves together?
- ✓ Is there any score in a game without people? Of course there isn't. Then which is more important, the people or the score?

To accentuate this point with older students, ask them to remember two years ago on this same date, "Do you remember the scores of the games you played that day?" They won't have a clue.

Then ask, "Do you remember who your friends were on that day?"Clearly the kids will see that people are more important.

Be very concrete with these examples. It is even useful to have the students point to each other and say, "You're the most important part of the game."

TEACHER: Point to a girl and say, "You're the most important part of the game." Point to a boy, a teacher, someone with ears, or wearing green and say, "You're the most important part of the game."

Begin applying these basic game principles to every part of the school day, so the carryover starts immediately.

In our culture it seems the adults have become so enamored with competition and entertainment that we have forgotten what is really important. How many parents have you seen run up to their child on the winning team and say, "It doesn't matter if you win or lose, it's how you play the game." They don't do that. As a kid you know you're a loser when you hear that speech. Our children have learned when our actions are not in harmony with the words "It's how you played the game."Creative Spirit is advocating that in school, people are most important, whether it's math, reading, science, or games.

Once your class rediscovers that people are the most important part of the game of school or life, you will be able to bring Healthy Play principles into your daily school curriculum. It's the full balance of the student's twenty or more answers on both posters that makes this program rich and meaningful. All we have to do as the teachers (elders) is to hold the children accountable to the values they have given. These are their answers. They just need countless opportunities to practice how to turn their beliefs into actions.

That's the philosophy: Play to have fun and people are the most important part of the game. It makes your role as the teacher simple. If all the students are playing, having fun, and taking care of the people, then keep playing. Everything is fine.

If your game resembles a battle of the gladiators or wrestlemania, then stop the game. The school curriculum does not designate you as the playground medic. Immediately bring your class together and calmly state, "This isn't what we put on our posters. If we can't play by our poster values, then our class game time is over for now. Do you want to keep playing? Then how are you going to fix it?"

Learning occurs each time the activity is *stopped* and the kids have to determine a solution. Don't always give the students the answers. Make them own the process and do the work. It's play. They can practice solving their problems. If the solution works, give them praise at the end of the activity. If their solutions don't work, halt the game completely (no more chances right now) and prepare to do something else in the daily curriculum. Hours later, or tomorrow, they will get another chance to show they're able to control themselves. You're not playing for entertainment, nor is ceasing play a punishment. It's part of school and learning.

The Healthy Play philosophy becomes a common language

your whole class can speak. The kids won't need doctorate degrees to implement these concepts. It works because they can master it. It works because they'll want a chance to enjoy being at school. It works because you'll enjoy teaching and having fun with your students.

Dealing with the Difficult Child During Poster Creation

Charlie and I are imagining that there are a good many of you who on reading the poster sections thought, "I have at least one kid, if not many, in my class who would answer, 'When I play, others get hurt. It's fun for me to hurt others.' I have at least one child who will put scoring high over people any day of the week." We've seen these children, and they can be frustrating and exasperating. They can also be comfortably managed.

Let's play out this scenario in a comic-book format:

WELL, I WANT TO THANK YOU FOR YOUR HONESTY, SKIPPY. HOWEVER, WATCH THIS.

RAISE YOUR HAND IF YOU THINK IT WOULD BE FUN TO BE HURT BY SKIPPY. WHO FEELS SAFE TO PLAY WITH SKIPPY?

HMM..

AS YOU CAN SEE, SKIPPY, NO ONE HERE FEELS SAFE TO PLAY WITH YOU. I KNOW THAT YOU WANT TO BE LIKED AND HAVE A LOT OF FRIENDS. YOU WILL HAVE GREATER SUCCESS MAKING FRIENDS IF YOU DON'T HURT THEM.

SKIPPY, I WANT YOU TO LISTEN CLOSELY TO THE RULES FOR THE FIRST GAME THAT WE ARE GOING TO PLAY.
YEAH, GOOD. I WANT TO PLAY.

I'D LIKE YOU TO PLAY, TOO. BUT, AFTER HEARING THE RULES I WANT YOU TO SIT BY THE BOUNDARY OF OUR GAME AND WATCH HOW THE OTHER KIDS PLAY WITHOUT HURTING EACH OTHER.
YOU MEAN I CAN'T PLAY?

YOU CAN'T PLAY UNTIL WE ALL FEEL THAT YOU WILL TRY TO PLAY WITHOUT HURTING OTHERS.
HMM

OH, I PROMISE! I PROMISE!

SKIPPY, JUST A MOMENT AGO YOU SAID YOU'D HURT OTHERS AND NOW YOU SAY YOU WON'T. I DON'T KNOW WHICH STATEMENT TO BELIEVE. WE DO WANT YOU TO PLAY, BUT WE WANT TO FEEL SAFE. IF YOU CAN WATCH THE FIRST ROUND OF OUR GAME WITHOUT DISRUPTION WE'D FEEL SAFER. WE ALSO COULD TRUST YOU BETTER. AFTER THAT WE'LL INVITE YOU TO PLAY WITH US AGAIN.

IT MAY FEEL LAME TO YOU, BUT HERE IN SCHOOL WE ONLY PLAY WITH THOSE WHO PLAY SO THAT EVERYONE CAN HAVE FUN WITHOUT GETTING HURT. I WANT YOU TO BE SUCCESSFUL IN MAKING AND KEEPING FRIENDS. WATCH ONE ROUND AND MAKE YOUR DECISION THEN AS TO HOW YOU WANT TO PLAY. REMEMBER, YOU CAN'T GO OFF TO ANOTHER PART OF THE PLAYGROUND. WE REALLY WANT YOU TO PLAY WITH US. MAKE A GOOD CHOICE.
THIS IS SO LAME!

DID YOU SEE HOW WELL THE GAME WENT WHEN WE PLAY IN A FRIENDLY MANNER? WOULD YOU LIKE TO JOIN US, SKIPPY? REMEMBER YOU MUST PLAY WITHOUT HURTING OTHERS.

At this point, we often assign another child to be Skippy's play buddy. His or her other responsibility is to watch and praise Skippy for positive behaviors and to gently remind him to modify his behavior if he begins to act out. Remember to keep all time-outs short or they will become ineffective. Thirty seconds to a minute is generally long enough. If the time-outs are too long, the children either feel punished or forget what they were given a time-out for. Remember age-appropriate attention spans.

Additionally, if one or more students persists with smart-aleck responses, announce to the class, "I don't think that we are ready to think about playing today. We'll try again tomorrow and see if everyone can be serious." This system of logical consequences will encourage support from the children who are behaving. You won't have to continue to bang your head against the wall. The children who were misbehaving will have their attention-seeking ploys backfire as they quickly discover their behaviors yielded no play-time for that day. Oops, back to math.

It is also possible that the child who is acting out could be moved to another classroom so that you can continue with the other children. Be sure to talk with the child one-to-one later, so you can assist him or her in learning acceptable social skills and behaviors, which will yield success.

The following suggestion will only work if you possess tact, compassion, a cool head, and solid mental-health skills. So, if a child who is acting out (usually trying to be the funny guy) is disrupting the poster creation in the classroom, we cautiously recommend the following technique when appropriate:

When a child is receiving negative attention for his comments that he thinks it would be okay to hurt someone, ask that child to come to the front of the class with you. Tell him that you are going to play out the possible consequences of his behaviors in a little skit. State that for a moment you agree with his rule that it is okay to hurt others. In fact, you envision and verbalize a scenario that you and this child were playing freeze tag. And, while you both were playing, you played by his rules and felt free to play real aggressively and hurt him. You hurt him so badly while playing tag that he broke his neck and was no longer able to move any part of his body from the neck down. He must now pretend to be paralyzed. Proceed to sit the child in a chair at the front of the classroom and continue the program. At first, you will have to remind him often that he can't move his hands or be able to play with the others when we do get outside because he is now paralyzed.

At the same time, remind the whole class that all this extra demonstration is wasting their valuable playtime. State that you don't mind going through this extra time-wasting material, but you would rather be spending the class's limited time playing. The rest of the class will unanimously agree that they don't want their time wasted and will start to enact the positive peer culture that we mentioned earlier. In addition to feeling the class's displeasure and pressure, the child who is acting out will realize that he won't get to play and will miss out on the fun if he doesn't modify his behavior quickly. Every time I've enacted this scenario, the child has quickly become more cooperative.

Remember that these ideas are just a few suggestions. Sometimes they'll work, and sometimes they won't. You might have a few ideas of your own. Be creative. Assess your and your children's needs. Try to discover the reason behind a child's acting out. It will often help you come up with a nonpunitive way of dealing with the problem presented.

When we play just to have fun, we create a nurturing environment for healthy relationships and a greater sense of personal and group pride. We begin to create community.

Rules

Knowing the two philosophical principles "We play to have fun" and "People are the most important part of the game," we find ourselves halfway to being able to use play therapeutically. We've identified the values we are going after with the creation of our posters. Now, to set up a safe environment on the playground and to practice and solidify these values, we must focus on two essential rules that you and your group must adhere to.

Rule 1

If anyone gets injured, whoever is closest to that person will stop and stay with him until he is ready to play again.

Remember Skippy? He was the child we introduced earlier who had difficulty being able to play without hurting anyone. There seems to be at least one Skippy in every class. He or she is the kid who, when playing a game of tag, has a hard time tagging others lightly. He seems to take great delight in tagging others with the force of a hurricane, leaving the bodies of his victims scattered throughout the playground.

Well, he's baa-ack. And, he's going to help us show how rule number one works, in comic-book format, as he receives feedback for his aggressive behaviors.

HA! GOT YOU, BOBBY. YOU'RE FROZEN!
OW!

SKIPPY!
OH BOY, TIME TO TAG SUZY.

SKIPPY, STOP! YOU HAVE TO TAKE CARE OF BOBBY. REMEMBER RULE #1. IF SOMEONE GETS INJURED. WHOEVER IS CLOSEST HAS TO STAY THERE AND TAKE CARE OF THEM. YOU CERTAINLY WERE THE CLOSEST WHEN IT HAPPENED. YOU'RE OUT OF THE GAME UNTIL BOBBY FEELS READY TO PLAY AGAIN.

I HATE THIS LAME RULE.

COME ON, BOBBY. STOP CRYING. YOU'RE OKAY. LET'S PLAY. THIS GAME IS GREAT AND I WANT TO PLAY.

YOU HURT ME, SKIPPY. YOU'RE MEAN AND KNOCKED ME DOWN.

IT WASN'T ME, IT WAS... SUZY. YEAH, THAT'S IT. IT WAS SUZY WHO KNOCKED YOU DOWN.

NO, IT WAS YOU, SKIPPY. YOU HIT ME REAL HARD AND KNOCKED ME DOWN. YOU HURT MY KNEE.

I'M SORRY. HERE LET ME HELP YOU UP SO I CAN GET BACK TO MY GAME.
I STILL HURT. I DON'T THINK I CAN PLAY YET.

C'MON BOBBY. DON'T YOU WANT TO PLAY?

I FEEL A LITTLE BETTER NOW. WALK ME TO THE DRINKING FOUNTAIN, SKIPPY. MAYBE I'LL FEEL READY TO GO BACK TO THE GAME AFTER I HAVE A DRINK.

OH, IF I KNEW THIS WOULD TAKE SO LONG BEFORE I COULD GET BACK TO PLAYING I WOULDN'T HAVE TAGGED HIM SO HARD

You've all seen this kid, Skippy. You probably know many kids like him. The number-one rule, "If somebody gets injured, whoever is closest to that person, *usually the person that injured the other person,* needs to stay and take care of that person," can change the dynamics for the child who demonstrates Skippy behaviors on the playground.

The kid who's a bully, like Skippy, is not going to learn nurturing skills right away, but he will be able to learn logical consequences. The exciting game that Skippy wants to play is going to turn into the carrot in front of the pony cart. To get to play, he will have to modify his behaviors. For instance, imagine it's the next day, and Skippy remembers that yesterday he was removed from the game because he had to take care of Bobby for fifteen minutes after hurting him. Bobby really does cry a long time, and the trip to the drinking fountain took another five minutes. At today's game of tag, Skippy is about to do another of his painful hurricane tags on Deanna when he has the following thought:

With this gentle system of logical consequences—play without hurting others and you continue to play, but if you hurt others you are removed from the fun to take care of the person you injured—kids like Skippy are going to start to learn (a little bit at a time) how to play with others more successfully. They will eventually learn, usually after only a few short times sitting out, that they can play the game without hurting anybody. They will learn to find greater satisfaction in making friends than in hurting others. And the wonderful thing about this program and this rule is that those kids who need to practice playing without hurting others get all the practice they need. Usually, they will practice over and over again until they get it.

For the child who knows how to nurture after accidentally hurting a peer, this rule provides a wonderful opportunity to foster and hone nurturance. As educators, mental-health professionals, or parents, we know that wonderful feeling and power that comes when you walk over to a crying child and he stops crying quickly because he feels better just being in our presence. It is so wonderful having this effect over hurt children, rescuing them from their pain by our mere touch, our mere presence. When we see a child who has been hurt by another, we swoop down out of the sky like Wonder Woman or Superman and take over the nurturing duties. But by being the local good Samaritan, we *rob the experience of nurturing* from the children who can learn from having accidentally hurt another. Turning the responsibility over to the children gives *them* a chance to practice nurturing. We give them a chance to share in the responsibility of making that person feel better. They become part of the healing. They learn personal responsibility and responsibility toward others. Responsibility belongs in every aspect of the school curriculum.

Remember, Charlie and I are nurses, and we're not advocating that you stand idly by, watching all the playground injuries that can occur in a day. "Oh, there's a lot of blood, gore, and guts out there, but those guys from Creative Spirit said in their book to make sure that the children do all the caretaking." No, no, no! Use your assessment skills. You know when you need to be there. You know when you need to be right up close and with a child. But give those kids who can take care of each other a chance to practice, and they will feel a sense of empowerment and a sense of caretaking that will help them become healthy, social beings.

Once again, the first rule of safety is that whenever somebody bumps a head, bonks an elbow, falls down, or is emotionally hurt, the closest person stays with that person and is out of the game until the injured party is ready to play again.

Have everyone in your class raise their hands if they can promise to follow this rule. Remember, this is how you continue to build your positive peer culture. If you have a child who can't promise—and you most likely will—firmly uphold the group's positive expectations, always acting nonpunitively. The child who cannot promise to play without hurting is instructed to watch the activity from the sidelines until you feel comfortable that he or she can join in without intentionally hurting others. Tell this child that everyone must be mindful and take care of each other. Let the child know that you'd prefer having him or her safely play, rather than watch the game. You might even verbalize that you want to help him learn the behaviors that will make him more friends. Your group of children is looking toward you for modeling and mentoring. You, as the local responsible elder, are going to hold the Skippys and all the people accountable for everybody's sake.

We've had teachers say that rule number one is a liberating concept because until it was adopted, every time they took care of two children that were hurt and had their back turned away from the other children, three more acts of aggression would happen. They saw themselves spending the whole recess treating, limit-setting, and mediating the entire playground. After being placed in this joyless position repeatedly, many teachers just stopped playing or facilitating play for their children.

Now, we give the power and responsibility back to all the children who demonstrate or need to learn successful social skills. Help the children and the adults to focus not just on scoring goals but on demonstrating that in our school community, the *people* truly are the most important thing. Making this concept of "people and caring first" a foundation for the entire curriculum, in and out of the classroom, we optimize all forms of learning and education.

When you ask your children, "When someone gets hurt, do you stay with him or run away?" the only acceptable response will be a resounding, "Stay with him!"

Rule 2

If two individuals have an argument or disagreement during a game, they must leave the game until their argument is peacefully settled.

The great thing about the Healthy Play program is its simplicity. Our second rule deals with the natural grist that occurs in almost every game: arguing. It is natural to have disagreements and to argue about them. What is critical is learning how to come up with a peaceful solution.

Arguing is not one of the reasons we play. It's not on the posters in the class. It's not fun. Therefore, since the arguers are not having fun, they must leave the activity until they can come back and enjoy the game as much as everyone else. Using this rule, we've taken the power away from those kids who can stop an activity every time they want to have an argument. From now on, they're the ones who need to go figure out a solution. This is a totally different way of thinking.

This rule and concept works because it continues to empower the students who are doing well. They are having fun, and with this system, the game goes on for them. The negative attention that so often accompanies arguments is now given minimal acknowledgment by the teacher and class. The teacher or any student can simply say, "If you two have an argument, take it out of the game." Only the two students involved leave. No gang of friends can accompany them. If more than two students disagree with someone, each discussion must be done by just two students at a time until everyone has had his say. By reflecting the disagreement back to the children, you coerce them to do the learning.

As always, the teacher or elder can join in to facilitate a productive, peaceful discussion. School rules about fighting or profanity are always in effect. Use your good judgment about when you are needed right on the spot between certain students to protect everyone's safety. In these cases, your wisdom is initially needed to model how a nonviolent argument is processed and possibly to prevent punches from being thrown.

On the other hand, you must let go of assuming the role of the absolute authority in resolving every child's dispute. Remember, it is during play that kids practice how to state their feelings.

Adults often say, "Just ignore Skippy when he's doing such and such." We have come to this useful insight after experiencing hundreds and hundreds of picky little squabbles and determining that most are certainly not worth fighting over. Let the students take similar steps, so they too can come to this realization. Don't get trapped into always solving problems for children, even though you can see the immediate wisdom of you solutions. When elders accept a responsible "stand back and watch" posture in conflict management, arguing becomes an educational experience for children.

One demonstration we like to share when we are setting up Healthy Play rules with students is the following:

Ask for a volunteer in your class, or pick a student at random. (We often recommend that you pick your "Skippy," who argues and is always seeking everyone's total attention.) Have this child come to the front of the room and face away from the class. Request that he do some diversionary task, such as watching the second hand and counting ten seconds on the clock out loud. Before Skippy begins to count, instruct the class to watch you *very carefully* while he's counting. As he counts, lightly tag him on the folds of his shirt or the sleeve so that he doesn't see you touch him or feel it. (I usually do something additionally distracting like point at the clock and ask Skippy if he's watching it carefully.)

After the ten seconds are up, have Skippy turn around and face the class. Tell the class that you were really setting up a demonstration about playing freeze tag and that now you want Skippy to argue with you about whether he is frozen or not. Loudly model each side of an argument.

TEACHER: I got you.
SKIPPY: No, you didn't.
TEACHER: Yes, I did.
SKIPPY: No way!
TEACHER: You're cheating!
SKIPPY: No, you're cheating!

Now introduce the new arguing rule as you and Skippy walk to the side of the class, pretending to leave the game so that you can continue your argument privately. Ask the class a question like, "Should we wreck your fun in this tag game because we're having a disagreement?" This will achieve the positive peer culture buy-in you are desiring when the class says, "No!"

Here's the real point of this demonstration. Inform Skippy that you are going to ask the class two questions. The first one is going to be bad news for him, but request that he hang in there because the second question is going to be real good news.

Question 1

TEACHER: Raise your hands if you saw me tag Skippy several times on the back while he was watching the clock. [*Almost everyone's hand goes up.*] So in this tag argument, I'm the honest one. I'm telling the truth that I got him. [*At the point, I usually model my most irritating "nah-nah" behavior and make a really big deal that I'm the honest person.*]

Before Skippy gets too defensive or has hurt feelings about this demonstration, quickly state, "I said I was going to ask a second question and that it will be good news for you."

Question 2

TEACHER: Raise your hand, class, if you have ever been tagged in a game but didn't feel it. [*Everyone's hand will go up on this question.*] So how many of you think Skippy is telling the truth in our argument and that he didn't feel me tag him? [*Many hands go up again.*] So you're telling me that Skippy is the honest one? That he's telling the truth? But you just said I was the honest one. You mean we are both telling the truth, and we are both being honest?

At this point the smoke detectors in the school may go off as the collective brain mass of your class has a complete meltdown over this unforeseen possibility of both people being honest and truthful in a disagreement. Both people are "right," for whatever that's worth. In reality, that's why they are arguing. The concrete conclusion you must now draw for the students is this: "How long do you want to spend out of the game arguing when you are both equally honest?" Now that everyone else who is having fun is still playing, let those with disagreements take as much time as they want to solve their problem. Ten seconds, ten minutes, the whole game time. It's their issue. Most choose to resolve problems very quickly. They would rather play. Most children will promptly learn what is worth arguing over and what is not.

Helpful Hints

1. Be clear that there is a specific area where those with disagreements must go and stay until resolution occurs. They may not go wandering off to do something else, which would probably be more fun. Failure to comply might have other consequences, such as missing tomorrow's games.
2. If one child doesn't want to talk, then both students still need to wait. Silent stubbornness is often an effective tool for children who haven't mastered verbal communication and are poised against a stronger peer. The stronger peer may learn that intimidation no longer works in this class because the other student's silence keeps them both out of the game. The children experience logical consequences in action. Sometimes you'll need to demonstrate flexibility. If one child truly makes attempts to solve the problem but the other child uses silence, manipulation, or noncompliance, you may let the compliant child return to the game. At this point, you can help the other child search for and learn more effective problem-solving techniques.
3. Don't be *sooooo* concerned about justice, liberty, and the pursuit of happiness in the outcome of two kids' argument. It's just a game! Just practicing how to stand close to someone with whom you disagree is an important skill. Creative Spirit does not advocate any one specific peer-mediation methodology. Most of these are fine, but we feel most kids aren't ready for a cookbook or step-program approach to happy endings. Here are the familiar basics:

   A. Look the person in the eyes.
   B. Speak in a calm voice.
   C. State your feeling about the issue by saying, "I feel ______ when you ______."

In reality, there are far too many adults who haven't got these skills mastered. For some children, just being ten feet away from an intimidating person is progress. This is school, and learning is a byte-by-byte (computer humor) process. Maybe next month the child will talk a little. Maybe two years from now, with daily practice, he will make some effective assertive statements. Kids aren't psychiatrists; they're just kids. Let the kids reach their own conclusions. Then, when it's really necessary to advance someone's learning, you can step in. (See next hint.)

4. Obviously, you are going to have students who must always get their way. First start the disagreement process on the peer-to-peer level, regardless of the outcome. Once you have spotted a dominating, manipulative, and recurring pattern, then you can use the same rule the kids are using to begin teaching some useful lessons to the dominator. Immediately after the two kids are finished, approach the dominator and inform him (it could be a her) that *you* want to argue with him. While you are arguing, you can address the real issues of social relatedness and making friends with the child who is ineffectively dominating his peers. You can help the child learn effective behaviors that will result in successful friendship. That's the real point. It is not who is tagged or not tagged.
5. Let a student stay out of the game in the designated watching area if he doesn't want to play or is too angry or upset to use the conflict-resolution process. Personal readiness often means removing oneself from a situation one is not ready for. The goal of these educational activities is not forced participation because everyone must be participating to be happy. You are not a bad teacher if kids are watching on the sidelines. You are just giving the students the time they need to compose their feelings safely. When they have settled down and are ready to resume having fun, they will let you know.

You may be thinking, "This sounds too easy. It's never going to work with my students." For some it won't. You'll always be needed as the teacher on the spot trying your best to help certain kids. Don't reject this concept because of the exceptions. What if it works on one student, or ten, or twenty-three? How much relief from this stress will help you each day? Just as the students learn in their reading, science, and math classes, they will become more effectively socialized each month that they practice this concept.

So those are the two rules: "Take care of anyone who is injured" and "If you have an argument, do it out of the game." Your role is to get into the middle of the game activities, so the kids can hear you praise them for doing well. Likewise, from the middle of the game, you can see which children need to be reminded of the rules and direct them to learn the proper behaviors. Now you are ready to go have fun.

A Little Processing Goes a Long Way

We need to address another very important aspect of the play activities. This activity nurtures and strengthens the values the children first named on their posters ("Why do we play?" and "What is the most important part of all games?") and later used in their playing.

Right after any activity session (whether the kids play one game or many), you must facilitate a short processing or dialogue session. Find a quiet area as far away from distraction as possible. These sessions should last between five and ten minutes each or longer if necessary.

Obviously, if you don't sit the kids down and quiet their excited energy, they will probably return to the classroom and bounce off the walls. This makes teaching difficult and no fun at all. But the main point of the processing session is to make the activities into more than cool games. This is the time to transform play into an effective tool for class management and school curriculum.

During the processing time, ask the children to identify only the positive experiences they felt or observed while playing. When students make complaints like "I saw Skippy cheat" or "You tagged me too hard," remind them that they should have dealt with those complaints *during* the games, using our rules and philosophies. Remind them, as often as needed, that the processing session is a time to discuss positive behaviors only. Left to their own devices, kids can become the kings and queens of put-downs, because that's what they've been taught. It's easy for them to find fault with themselves and others. They need your guidance to find the jewels within themselves and their peers. The processing session is an enjoyable way to do this.

Praising only positive behaviors helps make those actions, ideas, and values a reality in the children's lives. They experience that inner glow of personal joy and recognition. This is what helps children find their place within their own moral selves and positive peer culture. This positive peer culture tells kids how they must act if they want to be part of the fun and caring group. Active praise produces long-term internal change more effectively than most self-defeating "token" systems, which are rarely, at any practical length, found in the real world.

Although you, as the elder, will start the compliments and nominations (see the following hints), this process should very quickly become the children's responsibility. By doing this for themselves, the students create a self-perpetuating place where they feel the joy and satisfaction of a job well done.

Teachers have often told us that these after-games processing sessions become the highlight of the school day for both the students and themselves. The processing also carries over easily to other academics. This means greater group cooperation and teamwork because of the success of the individual child. Praising positive behaviors while reducing the emphasis on negative behaviors makes those positive behaviors the norm. It's a win-win situation for both the child and the class. These are the childhood experiences that help us succeed in our relationships, families, and jobs as adults.

Processing Techniques

One of the greatest sources of wisdom came to us not from any guru, teacher, or book. This piece of sage advice came in the form of the common railroad-crossing slogan: Stop, look, and listen. What great advice. Stop! Take the time to notice the world around you. Stop and truly *look* at what your world offers you. *Listen* to what it tells you. *Listen* to your heart and feelings. Awareness of self and others is the key to growth. If there is this much wisdom about railroad crossings, imagine the pearls of wisdom hidden within children and responsible elders.

The follow techniques are designed to help you cement positive behaviors with your group of children.

Nominations and Compliments

Our favorite form of processing uses the concept of nominations. After creating your posters and going over the rules, ask your kids if they know what a nomination is. This is a harder concept for kids to grasp than you might imagine. Many don't have a clue, so you may have to jog their media-prone minds and rephrase the question: "When I say I nominate someone, like 'I nominate Skippy,' what do I mean?" Usually at this point, their collective gears start turning, and you can almost see them visualizing their favorite musical group or actor accepting an award. Quickly a hand is raised, and someone says, "A nomination is, like, when you pick someone for, like, an award or something." Your response is, "Excellent. You're right. When you nominate people for something, you pick them and publicly announce their name and why you are choosing them. Today, and every time we play, we are going to watch each other and see who is doing all the wonderful things and values we listed on our posters. We are going to watch and remember which of our friends are playing fair and safe, who's taking care of the people when they bonk an elbow or fall down, because at the end of our playtime we are going to nominate them with a compliment. It might go like this: 'I want to nominate Julie because when she tags, she tags gently. Way to go, Julie. You take care of the people! I also want to nominate Suzy because when Xavier fell down, she stopped playing and immediately took care of him. She follows rule number one.'"

We recommend that immediately following each nomination you and the class reward the child chosen with a big round of applause. We make up all types of creative applauses and encourage the children to do so. Creative applauses such as "pinky," "spider," or "seal" applauses (use your imagination) further reinforce the positive behaviors growing in the group. Remember, if a child wants to talk about negative behaviors he saw, gently redirect him, explaining that "nomination time" is only for positive behaviors.

For children in kindergarten through second grade, you will probably have to replace the word *nominations* with *compliments.* Make sure these youngsters know what a compliment is before going out to play. Sadly, we have discovered that many five-, six-, seven-, or eight-year-olds have gotten this far in life without knowing what a compliment is. No wonder it's easier for them to put down people, including themselves, than to praise each other.

See, Hear, and Feel

Another technique to help children become more aware of their inner feelings is to ask them to identify positive things they saw, heard, or felt. Children will quickly say that they heard laughter and saw everybody having fun. This is great, as it publicly acknowledges the joy they've found and can achieve again. Soon they'll be able to identify more profound feelings. Verbalizing that one feels "happy" can evolve into "I feel joy when I feel accepted and part of our group," or " I feel safe that we can all play together without hurting each other." It is this acknowledgment of one's feelings that creates the self-awareness that motivates behavior.

Compliment Tag

Have you every tried to get a verbal response from your group of kids and gotten only that incredibly empty void? It's so quiet that you wonder if these are the same kids who were just screaming with joy mere seconds ago? Sure you have. Kids clam up sometimes. But we have an answer. Use the permission granted in Creative Play (coming up next), and turn your processing into another game. We play compliment tag, and it goes like this: I start by giving someone a compliment, and that makes him or her "it" (the leader of the current round). He or she, in turn, has to tag another person it by giving him a compliment, and so on. As the teacher, you may want to specialize your compliment for a child who is often overlooked or for a difficult child who did well. For example:

TEACHER: I want to compliment Zackery for staying with Israel when he fell. [*Everybody applauds.*] That makes you it, Zackery. Who are you going to tag with a compliment?

ZACKERY: I want to tag Lucy with a compliment because she plays fairly. You're it, Lucy. [*Applause.*]

LUCY: I want to tag Skippy with a compliment. He was able to play two out of our three games. He is really trying hard to play without hurting anyone. [*Applause.*]

SKIPPY: I want to tag Jeremy with a compliment because he is my friend and reminded me that I was tagging too hard. [*Applause.*]

The after-games processing is *essential* in increasing and cementing positive behaviors. Without processing, you will not garner the full benefits of the Healthy Play program. We encourage elders always to reserve five to ten minutes after activities for processing, to transform these really cool games into true tools of behavior reinforcement and consequence.

Quick Review

When we work with classes, we regularly review the basics before we go out to play. Remember, both children and adults learn and retain information by frequent repetition. We don't teach children in kindergarten the ABCs one day and expect them to memorize them instantly. We've never heard a teacher tell their kindergarten class, "Well, we just discovered the ABCs yesterday, so today we will read Melville's *Moby Dick.* And by the end of the week I'll be expecting your thesis about the grievous relationship between Ahab and the whale." Repeat the basics often or you'll lose them.

In rapid succession, before and after we play or at other spontaneous moments, we ask the four key questions:

TEACHER: The number-one reason we play is to have what?
STUDENTS: Fun!
TEACHER: Who is the most important part of the game?
STUDENTS: People!
TEACHER: If somebody gets hurt, do you stay with them or run off and play?
STUDENTS: Stay with them!
TEACHER: If you need to argue, do you do it in the middle or out of the game?
STUDENTS: Out of the game!

Introduction to the Continuum of Three Play Categories

Implementing the philosophy and rules found in this book will help you successfully teach basic social skills for your class and children. But that's just the starting point for using play as an effective learning tool in school. To maximize learning for both social skills and academics, let's focus on a continuum of three basic game concepts. Understanding these play dynamics will open exciting doors to bring play into your whole day's curriculum. For parents, knowledge of the game categories will help you customize activities for your children at home and in the neighborhood.

We humbly acknowledge that the basis for our continuum comes from particular concepts presented by the New Games Foundation, an organization founded in the early seventies dedicated to creating community through play. However, we have greatly expanded, updated, and reworked the concepts for behavioral and academic applications.

There are three categories in our continuum of game activities. The continuum starts with something we call creative or innovative play. That's the first basic idea. The continuum then advances to compassionate play. There has to be a level of compassion and trust in the activities that we do in each class, on the playground, in the cafeteria, or anywhere at school. Finally, *if appropriate,* we can explore the third concept, called soft aggression. It is a *continuum* of game dynamics, and we strongly recommend that you implement it in this order when you are working with your students. As with any educational process, you can't move the students to something more advanced until you and they have mastered the most basic information.

Creative Play

Creative or innovative play begins with the understanding that all games are made up. Yep, every game has been made up. The games weren't here in the earth's core when the planet was formed. Moses didn't climb the mountain, get the Ten Commandments, and receive a complete rule book of all games, including the special card games supplement as a bonus for his efforts. Every culture makes up games, and games are usually made up by people wanting to have fun.

Knowing this is a powerful tool. It empowers you and your class to use your imagination and creativity to make learning any subject more enjoyable. There are games for math, spelling, geography, and science. If you can't find what you need, then just make up your own.

It is useful to understand that there are really only six types of games. The first game type is follow the leader. Everybody plays this game. Just moments after you were born, you started playing one of the best games of follow the leader ever invented. The game is called smile. Mom (or Dad) held you in her arms and put a pleasant smile on her face. In a short time, once your eyes could focus, you learned to smile back. Then the real fun began, because you quickly discovered that your grandparents, siblings, uncles, aunts, cousins, and all sorts of other people knew how this game works. Advanced smile involves noses, eyes, and googy noises. But follow the leader doesn't stop there. By the time you're in kindergarten, you play this game with others when you skip, jump, wave your arms, and turn somersaults in succession. By middle school, follow the leader determines the shirts and shoes you buy, the songs you like, and the movies you see. We keep playing follow the leader all our lives. For adults it's the cars we buy and where we go on vacation, but mostly, we evolve our follow-the-leader game into the laws we want. If your leader is a benign one, this is a great and valuable game.

The second basic kind of game is tag. The world's most complicated form of tag is called baseball. Baseball is nothing more than tag. The baseball is it. You knock it somewhere, and you run to base, where you are safe. Anything with a base where you are safe sounds like tag to me. And if you get tagged with the ball before you reach base, you're out. That's the rule somebody made up. Other rules make baseball a more complicated form of tag. Foul balls count as strikes. Well, they count as strikes unless it's your third strike, and then they don't count as a strike unless you were trying to bunt. If this happens, then a foul ball does count as your third strike. Those are rules that *people* made up to have *fun.* And when working in elementary, middle, or high school, we can make up the rules the way we want, to have our own fun. When our goal is education, self-esteem, and values, different ideas can be made up that meet these needs.

The next basic game is keep-away. They say that the American attention span is dwindling, but we don't believe it. Each year Americans can watch a twelve-hour marathon of keep-away on New Year's Day. That kind of attention span is awe inspiring. In the fall, Americans watch three hours of keep-away every Monday night, formally calling it football. Football is really no more than a complicated version of keep-away. It's still a relative of pickle in the middle. Basketball is also keep-away, but you dribble the ball. Hockey is keep-away on ice. Soccer is keep-away, but you kick the ball. Once you get the idea that there are only a few basic types of games, you can see where people's imaginations take over to make games better and more interesting.

The fourth kind of game is capture. Chess, checkers, and cards are typical capture games. Here, a bigger or more valuable piece usually captures something smaller. The values of kings and queens associated with the chess pieces or cards were made up to reflect the medieval world the people lived in. What if cards represented foods? A glass of milk might capture a candy bar. Bread could move farther than soda pop if they were based on the RDA guidelines.

Logic puzzles are the next basic style of game. These activities are based on intellect. An important part of the overall Healthy Play program is using a wide variety of activities, which highlight all the different talents students possess. In your class, you will have kids who are good at running and jumping. Other students will be whizzes at solving puzzles. Some children will be imaginative and creative, while others may become your rule developers. At every grade level, we've seen future diplomats and doctors at play. Solving logic puzzles using cooperation and teamwork will let all the students stretch their minds and learn while having fun.

The sixth kind of game is accumulation: Whoever gets the most of something is the winner. Monopoly must be the ultimate accumulation game. If you get all the hotels and all the money, you've accumulated the most, and therefore you win. Most video games are just point-accumulation activities, often with a lot of graphic violence. What we'd like to do in Healthy Play activities is accumulate people. When you've accumulated all the players in the game, everyone wins. The more the better, and with this format, students' feelings won't be hurt, because they are never eliminated from the game.

The basic premise behind the concept of creative play is that *all* games are made up. So we can simply change the rules, titles, or other features of any game to meet the needs of the individuals playing. Let's use the following scenario as an example of how we can use a rule change to meet the needs of a particular individual. Imagine that I'm working with this class, and one child is the class scapegoat. None of the other children want to include this child in any of their games. He's got "a way high cootie factor." The game we're playing is safety haven (see page 67). To keep from being tagged it, children need to hug and hum with another child. As you might imagine, no one wants to hug our scapegoat friend. Nobody wants to touch this cootie-filled kid, much less hug and hum with him. But I happen to notice that this ostracized child is one of only two children who are wearing the color purple this day. So I stop the game momentarily and change the rules. "Now in our game of safety haven," I say, "you're only safe hugging and humming with somebody who is wearing the color purple." Instantaneously, the children rush off to seek safety with the new "safe" children, to avoid being tagged it. Without much thought, our scapegoat child quickly becomes their safe port in the storm. Automatically, the most unpopular child suddenly, almost magically, becomes one of the two most popular children. Without abstract processing, which rarely works with children, "cootie" components are shattered and behaviors changed.

Or you might want to reinforce the number four to your kindergarten class. So during safety haven, you change the rules. You are now only safe hugging in groups of four children. Now you have a kinetic and visual way of reinforcing the children's understanding the number four.

These are but a few examples of how you can use the concept of creative play to meet the various needs of your group of children. There are many other ways, such as the following, to make games much more successful by using the concepts of creative play.

Keep Safety the Number-One Focus

The number-one way to make games more successful is to keep them safe. The one rule that I wish I had in my neighborhood when I was growing up is that hard tags just don't count. You remember those hurtful tags. Bam! Those kinds of tags often knock people down or bring tears to their eyes. Well, they no longer count! And not only do they not count, if you tag hard and just happen to knock somebody down, you have to stay with him according to rule number one. You're out of the game until he feels better and can play again. Combining hard tags with rule number one becomes a very powerful tool, and we encourage all parents and teachers to change to safer styles of tagging.

Other suggestions for making games safer focus on appropriate touching or tagging with appropriate body parts. When we play triple tag (see page 65), for example, we state that tagging others with our feet or knees doesn't count, because this would be more likely to seriously hurt them. We have permission now to change the game to make it safer. *All* children want to feel safe.

Reward Teamwork to Foster Cooperation

You can reward teamwork with bonuses or praise. You can even play a traditional game. Let's say you are doing a traditional game of basketball, but you want to create a greater sense of cooperation and sharing with your group of kids. Imagine we have two teams. Both teams have been told, "Hey, if you guys can all share the ball so that everyone gets a chance to play and make a basket, your team will get a fifty-point bonus." Team one says, "We don't need your stinkin' fifty points." Team one has Betty, Janet, Al, Roger, and Angie. They're one really hot basketball team, and Janet just happens to be the school's best player. The kids at school say she'll be the next Michael Jordan. This is how team one's kids play:

Every time one of them gets the ball, it goes automatically right to Janet because Janet is their hotshot player and high scorer. Clearly, in their minds, if Janet gets the ball, she'll make all their points, and they'll score higher than team two. It doesn't seem to matter that no one but Janet really gets to play on their team. True to form, Janet performs well and has scored all of team one's thirty-six points.

Over on team two we have Cathy, Lori, Muriel, Susan, and Shirley. Team two buys into the fifty-point bonus and adopts the attitude that says, "Let's go for the fifty points. Let's try really hard and share." And so they go about playing well and share the basketball. Cathy is a really good basketball player. So are Lori, Muriel, and Susan. In fact, they have all made their baskets and need only Shirley to make hers to get that fifty-point bonus. But for Shirley to make a basket, she has to stand on just the right spot on the court. The sun has to be behind her, and the wind can't be blowing too hard. In fact, Venus has to be aligned with Mars for Shirley to make a basket. Team two still wants that bonus and will have to help Shirley by providing her a perfect setup shot. All of a sudden, Lori gets the ball and gives it to Shirley. Her team roots for her: "Go Shirley, get that fifty points." Oh, the pressure. Because she is not known for her basketball skills, this is the first time Shirley has had a basketball in her hand for the whole school year. In fact, having a basketball in her hands is so rare that she momentarily stops the game as she ponders what the word *Voit* might mean and why basketballs are so bumpy. Returning from her daze, she shoots, but the ball doesn't make it anywhere near the hoop. Still, she had the ball in her hands, and it was real exciting. So the game continues a little longer. This time teammate Cathy gets the ball back to Shirley. Shirley gets it. Having the ball twice in her hands may actually qualify as practicing now. Wow, she's had the ball twice within a five-minute period. "Go Shirley, get that fifty points," shout her teammates. She throws. There it goes, bouncing off the backboard. Third time, teammate Muriel sets it up. The perfect setup for Shirley. Shirley throws it up, and the ball appears to move in slow motion. From an unidentifiable source we hear the theme music from the *Chariots of the Gods* as, whoosh, the ball gloriously goes in. Suddenly, team two, because they decided to play cooperatively, is now winning sixty to thirty-six. And the child who is often ridiculed for poor skills becomes the hero, the fifty-point player. Creative use of scoring, rewards, and praise become other ways to foster cooperation.

Have Multiple Its

Another thing you can do to improve total participation and excitement is to have multiple its in a game. If there's just one person chasing after another person, your game of tag becomes quite boring for most of the participants. Kids are ego focused. They want the world to revolve around them. This is not good or bad. It is just where they are developmentally. Let's accept, respect, and honor this. All kids want to be playing all the time. When you have multiple its, everybody stays involved.

In fact, having multiple its makes it easier for players of differing abilities to play the same game together. A child in a wheelchair becomes equal with chairless children in a game of safety haven. With many people tagging, the playing field expands into a joyfully chaotic arena where mercy tags for the physically challenged are eliminated. With multiple its, the superstar athlete is humbled as another child with less athletic skill can tag her. No one needs to play up or down to another. We recommend one it for every six to eight people. Or play "Like, totally it" tag, where everyone is it at the same time.

When using multiple its, you'll need to come up with identifying markers, so everyone will know who is it. We like to use bandannas. We play down their power as gang colors and just turn them into simple reminders of who's it. If colors are too controversial on your campus or in your neighborhood, you can easily substitute paper towels. Use anything you want: bandannas, paper towels, stuffed animals, balls, bean bags, torn-up sheets, whatever.

Alter the Game Speed

Imagine a game of "Like, totally it" tag (see page 63). Maybe the children are so excited that some have become reckless and others end up not feeling safe. Creatively change the speed, so that instead of running, players are instructed to move heel to toe. This means that children have to slow down to carefully and sequentially touch the heel of one foot to the toe of the other as they move through the playing field. We might have them jump on one foot. The game slows down, becoming safer, and still maintains excitement.

Maybe the game is going too fast. A traditional round of "Like, totally it" tag usually lasts less than a minute. Walking heel to toe instead of running makes your thirty-second game now last two or three minutes. Change the rules to make the game safer or more enjoyable.

Add More Bases

You might want to add more bases to your games. Let's alter the traditional game of kick ball. Imagine seven bases instead of four. I'm up at bat, poised to kick. With seven bases, I, who am not the greatest kick-ball player, would now have three additional chances of getting on base. Who says it has to be just four bases?

In fact, when we play kick ball, we eliminate all the problematic rules to make the game more fun for the people playing. Foul balls are boring and waste a lot of time. So foul balls now count even if you kick the ball behind you into the backstop instead of toward the outfield. And who says you have to run to the right? Maybe you could opt to go the other direction around the bases. There are few things more fulfilling than seeing a child who never gets on base score a seven-base home run because the ball just tapped his foot and he faked everyone out by running to the left instead of the right. All any adult or child wants is to feel successful at play. All we want to feel is that everyone here is our friend and that we're not going to feel humiliated or intimidated. We just want a chance to play. By creatively altering the rules of kick ball, the children who want to play it traditionally can do so, while other children can celebrate their humanity and their abilities by being included.

The most exciting aspect of creative play is when the kids take over the process. We just finished working at a school where we taught some fifth-grade students seven-base kick ball. The kids' eyes and minds went wide open when they discovered the freedom to make games better. By the next week, when we returned to the school, we discovered they had already invented their own game of double-pitch kick ball. Two pitchers simultaneously pitch to two kickers, and both players kick their own ball and run opposite directions around the bases. The base runners must coordinate their base-running strategy so that they can touch hands at second base and at home in order to score. If either base runner is tagged out, then both of them are out.

This is an example of what every teacher should let his or her class achieve with creative play. Let the students own this process by trying out their new ideas. These fifth graders had immediately begun to use creative-play concepts to establish how to make up rules they all would follow. This bonded the class together with a vital sense of cooperation toward their common goal. This was a real, hands-on, action learning experience that didn't come from reading about self-esteem or peer mediation. The game was just the fun vehicle for useful curriculum.

Change the Number of Balls in a Game

When we play soccer, we usually use three to five Nerf soccer balls. There's so much more action going on for everyone when you add more balls. With only one ball, it's usually the gifted soccer players who get to play and run around. Occasionally, some of the other children get to play, but they're pressured to turn the ball back over to the best players, who will do the scoring. In general, the majority of the students just stand around during the game. Not any longer.

With multiple balls in play, the superstar players tend to congregate around one ball, trying to offset the other team's best players. But now there is a second ball waiting for the average players to try their best. There's even a third ball. Students who almost never get a chance to play are now kicking and passing a ball to other classmates. Every student now gets to develop a stronger heart, lungs, and muscles and better coordination. Given a chance to actually play, all students have an opportunity to develop their bodies and improve their skills.

When there are three or more balls in play, there is more action and a lot more scoring. A hidden benefit of so much action is that no one can follow the score. The teacher can begin accenting the point that the class is just playing for fun, and no one really needs to worry about scoring. The majority of students will see the point.

Creative play often contradicts the modeling we see in our adult culture. As a society, we pressure our kids into team sports at the earliest possible age. In reality, kids have not matured enough for these highly developed team games. Experts in child development have found that children aren't ready for team sports until middle school or even high school.

At the appropriate developmental age, children can master in weeks what they have been pressured into trying to do for years. Their maturation process must move beyond the very self-centered, ego-focused period of their life before they can achieve success with team concepts. This egocentric period of life is not a bad thing. It's just part of being a child. At ages six to eleven, children are rarely part of a team. They merely wear the same color shirt as everyone else. In elementary-school settings, it is important to acknowledge that each and every child just wants to play with the ball. "My turn" is their focus. Put extra balls out there and every student will learn to play.

Change the Boundary Size

Let's play the game of "Like, totally it" tag, which we mentioned earlier. Here every player in the game is it. Envision you are going to play this game in a space the size of half a basketball court. Thirty students will freeze almost everyone playing in less than ten seconds. By doubling the arena and playing on a full basketball court, the game will last twenty to thirty seconds. The added space also means the game is much more physically active. There is now more space to run in. Pretend you want to play this same game on the football field. The children have lots of space in which to avoid being tagged. There will be lots of long-distance running for the players. The game can now last a long time, or maybe too long. Players who get frozen early could be stuck standing for five or more minutes while the others run around. This could be boring. On the other hand, if *every* student in the *whole* school played at once, you might find the football field is the perfect size for the number of people.

Boundary size allows you and the class to control the amount of action. Use this dynamic to promote safety in games when students are running too fast and having too many collisions and injuries. Make the game space smaller if need be. If the kids want more action, consider that the boundaries can be increased, but the students are responsible for not crashing into each other and hurting themselves. Learning to play is an educational process for practicing personal responsibility.

Expand your creativity. Boundaries don't have to be squares, rectangles, or circles marked by lines or cones. In Arizona, where the temperature often reaches 100 degrees or more, one teacher found a great solution for her class's tag game. The shaded area of two big trees became the playing space. Students eagerly complied with these strange boundaries. More important, the teacher imaginatively used the game for a science experiment. Student groups were asked to predict when the playing area was going to be at its maximum size based on the sun's position and the amount of shade. They then tested their predictions and also measured the temperature difference between shady and sunny areas. This academic exploration of boundaries could also include math. Try having your class calculate the number of square feet in playing areas of various sizes. As often as possible, involve practical crossover academic learning experiences in your games. These concrete examples make sense to young minds.

Change the Focus of Scoring

At almost every, no, at *every* school we have visited there are classes where score keeping has become a major problem. The conflicts and arguments about scores have led many exhausted teachers to give up playing completely. Totally abandoning all play is not an effective learning solution for children at school. As always, your first approach should be to use your class posters to point out why the class is playing. Sometimes this works immediately, but more often this refocusing on the social-skills concept of play takes weeks or months before it makes a serious impact on the kids who are determined to act out. So try using our arguing rule. The next time your class goes to play, have the students who disagree about the game's score move to the side, where they can argue while everyone else gets to play a new game. If this doesn't work, have the class vote to ban score keeping out loud. Anyone announcing the score at the end of playtime will miss some or all of the next day's play. Rules like this should initially last a maximum of only a day or two. That way the students can soon try again to see if they can control themselves. If problems persist, slowly increase the scoring-ban time frames to one or two weeks. Some teachers have banned scoring for the whole school year, and students very quickly seem not to miss it. They just like that they still get to play and can now do so without headaches from constant bickering over the score.

One of the more imaginative solutions to scoring that we have developed is something called the single-digit score. With this concept, a team's score can never exceed a single-digit number. Therefore, a 9 becomes the best score either team can ever achieve. Once your score reaches or exceeds 10, you reduce it to a single digit by adding the numbers together. Example: A score of 10 becomes 1 + 0 = 1. A score of 23 becomes 2 + 3 = 5.

This really changes game strategy. If you were winning 9 to 5 and you score that tenth point, your score changes, and now you find your team losing 5 to 1. The kids will quickly see this new challenge when someone like Skippy, the class home-run hitter, is up to bat. Bases are loaded, but all of a sudden everyone wants him to make an out. Being competitive has new tactics. Or maybe Skippy is the kid who always makes the out. Now his team is grateful that it's his turn because he will keep their score right where it is, at 9. Single-digit scoring presents new possibilities for everyone and a lot less emphasis on the score. You may find there are more tie games and you're practicing math.

Another scoring solution is to play games where the ultimate score is achieved by pitting the whole class against itself. This is like playing the whole class against time. Games like magic shoe (page 69) can be easily timed. If yesterday the class did the game in one minute and forty-three seconds, can the class do it today in less time?

Eventually your class may be able to play magic shoe in team format. Have relay races where the challenge is to determine what the fastest-slow time can be in the class. For example, team A has the fastest four players that do the race in 15 seconds, each for a total of 60 seconds. Teams B and C each have four medium-speed players that each do the race in 30 seconds for a total of 120 seconds. Team D has the four slowest players at 45 seconds each for a total of 180 seconds. When the race is done the first time, the slowest-slow time of 180 seconds is achieved by team D. If the teams are redivided so that each team has a 15-second racer, a 30-second racer, and a 45-second racer, teams can then achieve the fastest slow-time of 120 seconds.

In this format, the students quickly discover that putting all the speedy kids on one team and all the slowest on the other gives the class the slowest-slow time. They will need to balance everyone's abilities so that all the teams are equal. Only then can they achieve the fastest-slow time combination. The most gifted athletes will still be the fastest, but the other students will not feel ostracized or embarrassed in front of the whole group. Because everyone can comfortably join the activity, the class as a whole will get stronger and healthier, and the fastest-slow time will keep getting better.

Encourage Others to Offer Suggestions

Make everyone feel comfortable about offering suggestions or ideas. In class, every student has valuable ideas to contribute from time to time. Play is an area in which children should feel free to practice sharing their notions without fear of being laughed at by their peers. Initially, put-downs by some students may occur. Be prepared to use your class peer-pressure system to establish an environment that allows everyone the freedom to be heard. If problems persist, you can use the arguing rule to discuss with a specific student that hurting someone else's feelings is not part of why the class plays.

Voting is an essential part of our democracy. Games can give the students daily practice in voting their beliefs. Let's go back to "Like, totally it" tag. Your class may have a student who asks, "What happens if two people touch at the same time?" The usual adult response is to answer the question and then dictate a rule. From now on, allow the kids to vote. "How many agree that both people are frozen together? How many feel that when two players touch it should cancel out and neither person is frozen? Today we are going to play with the rule such-and-such, which the class voted for."

Often it's great to model minority rights. "Tomorrow let's try the rule change the other way, and then we can see if we like one way better than the other. Maybe both ways will be just as good, only different." Don't be afraid to try ideas that you (the elder) know probably won't work unless they are obviously unsafe. Help children get comfortable with trying ideas, so they get to experience the outcome of their decisions. When a classroom community views failures as successful learning experiences, there will be no stopping their potential to use imagination and creativity.

Pick Teams Randomly

Ahhh! Picking captains who pick teams. Could the adults of this world create anything more psychologically painful for the majority of students' self-esteem than this process? We set up problems and failures before we even leave the classroom to play a game. The captains always pick certain peers first. These honored few, of course, think this method is great. They always get a big self-esteem boost for being well-known or respected athletes. However, the last dozen kids picked always feel horrible.

In your school, do you pick teams for reading or math? How about spelling, science, or art? What a change that would be. "Oooh, oooh! We want Skippy on our team. He never misses a spelling word. We'll all get A's this week." Of course you don't do this. Then why should we treat the area of play so differently?

No child comes to class thinking, "I can't wait till 10:30, when we play kick ball and I get to be the last one picked because no one wants me because I always make outs." It's no wonder so many children avoid these negative experiences by playing sick, acting out, making fun of someone else worse than them, starting an argument, or sitting down and just not joining the game. These are the signs of children trying to protect their self-concept. As educators, we must realize that children genetically mature at such varying rates. In any third-grade class some children seem as physically advanced as fifth graders. Others have matured more slowly and are like first graders. It's not something the children can control. No one should be penalized for having a different genetic time clock than another person. To make life easier for everyone, swiftly give up using captains.

The solution for making up teams is called the double divide. Here's how picking equal teams works.

Step One

Have everyone in class pick a partner. Children without partners put a hand in the air and look for others who aren't partnered. Save yourself (as the elder) from being partnered until the students are all matched up. This way, on days when you have an even number of students, you will not get a partner. On the days when the total is an odd number, you will get a partner.

Step Two

Let the partners choose between two objects—for example, between the Nile River and the Amazon River if you happen to be studying large rivers of the world. Every partnership now must have one person choose to be either the Nile or the Amazon. Now you ask for all those students who picked the Nile to raise their hands. Quickly check to see that each partnership has one hand up. Have all the Nile partners go to one side of the play area. Have all the remaining Amazon partners go to the other side. Like magic, you will have two equal teams chosen without captains. No one's self-esteem is harmed.

Will some students try to manipulate this process? Of course they will. If they don't divide fairly and quickly, send the partners to the side of the game to have their disagreements settled. Let the game begin without them. Always keep empowering the healthy peer culture in your class by starting the game up for them. Once your class students have played a month or more with creative-play concepts, they will understand that being on a certain team really doesn't matter. The rest of the year will be wonderful.

Obviously, this process can work for whatever number of groups you need. If you want four groups for a science project, have your class get into partnerships of four. Pick four options: winter, spring, summer, fall. Then have the groups complete the double, now quadruple, divide.

Sometimes, don't divide up the children. This will keep them guessing your intentions and reduce manipulations. At other times, use creative-play concepts to divide by birth dates, height, people with siblings and those without, people with dogs as pets, those with cats, and so on. Most of the games in this book do not need even teams. So don't worry if the teams are not always even. See instead that the game is played safely and fairly.

These ideas become the basic dynamics for creative play. Together with you, your students, and your curriculum, they will provide daily opportunities to put more fun and joy into being and learning at school.

Creative/Innovative Play Activities

"LIKE, TOTALLY IT" TAG

(All grades, any number of players, large playing area, no equipment)

How It's Played

This is the ultimate freeze-tag game and a perfect place to start focusing on playing fair. Set up a playing area and make sure everyone knows the boundaries. In this game, *all* the players are simultaneously it. The rules are simple. Whoever touches another

"Like, totally it" tag

person first, freezes him. When two people tag at the same time, both players are frozen. Once they're frozen, they stay that way until the game ends. Play continues until only a few players are left unfrozen (about six). At that point, have everybody who is frozen yell out a five-second countdown to indicate the game is coming to an end. To make sure everyone has a "toada-lay awe-sum" time, humorously explain this game in your best Valley girl (or boy) accent. This is a fast game and a good one for exploring what effect different-size boundaries have on a game. Play it many times before moving on to something else.

The Gift of the Game

Traditional freeze tag had its moments, but they often were too short and enjoyed by too few. Remember being it, with that impossible task of freezing all the players? You could try to tag your friends from now till next December and still never accomplish your task. And remember standing around feeling wistful and uninvolved as the person who was it went after one solitary runner on the other side of the playground? Boring! You could only get into the action when, and if, you were noticed by the person who was it. "Like, totally it" tag changes all that, dudes and dudettes. Players shine even before the game begins as everybody is encouraged to call off the name of the game in their best Valley accents (highlighting all children's attributes of humor and acting).

This is the game we usually start with when playing with a new batch of funsters. This game sets the tone for *all* the liberating game experiences that can and will occur. This is the ideal game to equalize *all* the players right from the get-go. Everybody gets a chance to play. No waiting. No need to take a number. Immediately, participants experience and will easily buy into Creative Spirit philosophy and rules with this activity. "Like, totally it" tag becomes one of your strongest marketing tools when initiating the Healthy Play program in your class. All the socialization dynamics that hook a person into wanting to play in a healthy manner are introduced at once: acceptance, equality, total participation, fairness, excitement, safety, compassion, humor, and fun. "Like, totally it" tag is the one to start with!

TRIPLE TAG

(All grades, a large playing area, no equipment, any number of players)

How It's Played

Set up boundaries for your playing area. All players are it and may tag any other player. What makes this game different from "Like, totally it" tag is that kids must be tagged three times before they're frozen solid. The first time a student is tagged he must hold the spot where he was touched with one hand. The second tag forces him to use his other hand to hold that spot. (Now that both of his hands are occupied, he can tag players with his head, elbow, or body. Feet or knees may *not* be used for tagging because of safety concerns.) The third tag freezes that player solid.

Play continues until only a few players are left unfrozen (about six). At that point, have everybody who is frozen yell out a five-second countdown to indicate that the game is coming to an end.

The Gift of the Game

What's in a name? Plenty! When we first observed this game on playgrounds, it was called hurt, wounded, and dead or hospital tag. It was clear the players tried to make the game live up to its name. The game was played in an aggressive style, and children did consciously try to hurt one another. In fact, if you want your children to play like gladiators or reenact scenes from the local ER, have them play hospital tag. We suggest instead that you play triple tag. It's the same game, but the name conjures up playfulness and not scenes of mass destruction with wounded bodies scattered on the playground. Names have power. Names of games can suggest expected behaviors.

Names also can help groups of different ages buy into the activities. For instance, there is a game called Noah's ark, which involves kids mimicking an animal (for example, hopping like rabbits) to find the partner who shares their same animal name. It really is a delightful game. When we play it with church groups and young children, we play it as Noah's ark. However, when we play it with teenagers and adults, we play it as the mating game. Ooh! It's still the same game, but the mating game sounds less childish to teens and adults. They're more open to your suggestion of this game. In fact, don't tell older kids that broken wheel (page 88) is an advanced form of duck, duck, goose. They might become resistant to this game with that information. Older children would miss out on a fun activity because they were turned off by the name of the game. Never forget that "naming" is important and sets the tone for desired behaviors.

SAFETY HAVEN

(Kindergarten and up, eight to fifty players, indoors or outdoors, bandannas or markers to identify the players who are it)

How It's Played

This is a special tag game in which the participants are only *safe* when they seek *haven* with each other. Decide how large a playing area you will need, and call everyone's attention to the boundary lines. Have several players selected as it (one for every six to eight players), and give them the identifying markers. Players disperse throughout the playing area, and the game begins. If a player who is it tags another player, itness is then transferred from the original it to the person who was tagged. The identifying marker is also transferred to the new it, so everyone can easily see the change in roles. Players may choose to run around to avoid being tagged, or they can seek safety haven (a safe moment of freedom from being tagged it) with another player by hugging her or him as the two of them hum together. Their safe period lasts only as long as it takes to hum together on *one* breath. After their humming breath is out, they must find a *new* person to hum and hug with or risk being tagged.

Variations during this game keep it fresh. Feel free to change the safety haven rules. Try being safe only when hugging people wearing green, for instance, or when hugging in groups of four or with someone who likes broccoli.

The Gift of the Game

Students of all ages, and especially teenage ones, have few opportunities to socialize and play together in a positive manner. It seems as if touching has been reduced to only two types in our society: erotic and violent. This is truly unfortunate, for human beings, especially children, need to experience all the types of appropriate touching to develop physical and emotional intimacy. The beauty of safety haven is that this activity facilitates appropriate touching

Safety haven

within a safe public area. Since everyone is a potential safe base, the game also makes everybody of equal worth as a safe port in a storm of fun.

With simple modifications to the rules, a teacher can make the class scapegoat or a withdrawn child the most popular child in the room. For example, the first time I worked in Ms. Demsey's third-grade class, it was immediately obvious which child was the scapegoat. The taunting was merciless and mean-spirited. Once outside, I noted that the class would avoid seeking a safe haven with this student. Other students would not hum or hug with him. All the other students kept this child as an underdog so they could feel like overdogs. Wanting to break through this trust-defeating dynamic, I happened to notice that this child was one of three children out of thirty who had a cartoon printed on his T-shirt. Using the freedom of creative play, I changed a rule. I told the children they would be safe only if they were to seek haven by hugging and humming with a child who had a cartoon drawing on his shirt. As if by magic, the child who was the least popular immediately became one of the three most popular children in that class. The cootie factor shattered, and from that point on, this child was included as an equal player, even when the rules were changed to share the hugs, hums, and safety havens with other children.

This same creative-play dynamic works equally well with shy and withdrawn children. I learned from another teacher that five-year-old Lori avoided all activities, day after day, by sitting on the sidelines because she was afraid of being rejected by the other children. True to form, on the day that I came to her class, she refused to enter any game I initiated even though she was often invited. She was the only child wearing glasses that day, so for twenty seconds the rule was changed to have the children seek haven with those wearing glasses. Well, the mountain came to Mohammed as all the children embraced Lori, showering her with their laughter, hugs, and melodically silly humming. Her smile and laughter were evidence enough that her fear of others had melted away. It was this delightful invitation from her peers that mobilized her to participate. After experiencing those twenty seconds of success, she joined in the rest of the games.

MAGIC SHOE

(Kindergarten to second grade, indoor or outdoor walking space, no equipment, any number of players)

How It's Played

This is a great game to begin developing trust and cooperation in younger children. Have each child take off one shoe (ooohhh, it stinks!) and balance it on top of her head. Each magic shoe should be balanced on its owner's head, so she can move around. Players practice walking around while trying to keep their shoe from falling. Now have everyone line up across one side of your playing area. The object is to walk about twenty-five feet to the other side without having the magic shoe fall off their heads. If it does

Magic shoe

fall, the child becomes frozen. But that's no problem. Any other unfrozen child can come over and help by stooping down and picking up the magic shoe fall and giving it back to its owner. (The group can vote on whether the child who is helping must balance her own shoe on her head with or without her hands while picking up the other shoe.) Once the shoe has been replaced on the head from which it fell, the frozen player can move again. To make the activity more challenging, see how fast the group can help everyone get to the opposite side. If this proves successful, try going over and back. Can the class beat the best time they've ever done? Can they walk backward? How about with their eyes closed? Make up lots of new rules.

The Gift of the Game

We like this game so much because kids like it a lot. This is one of the silliest activities that adults experience at our trainings, and at first some are reticent to walk around with shoes on their heads. But kids understand the pure silliness of taking off that smelly old shoe and placing it on their heads. Children won't hide their willingness to believe in the shoe's magic power. Adults often only see tilted heads with intensely crossed eyes and tips of tongue stuck out of the corner of mouths as children strain to keep the shoes balanced on their heads. The gift is to remember doing things that children like to do. Do things that adults may feel extra silly doing. Enjoy and stay open to the delight of regressed and innocent beings. They have much to teach us.

GHOST

(Kindergarten and up, any number of players, large playing area, no equipment)

How It's Played

Have all players form a circle holding hands. (Process any problems like hand squishing or arm pulling.) Pick four ghosts, place them in the center of the circle and have them pretend to go to sleep. The remaining players begin to walk clockwise around the ghosts while counting out loud the hours of a clock from one o'clock to midnight. At "midnight," players let go of each other's hands and run away from the ghosts that are waking up. Upon awakening, ghosts wave their arms high in the air while making ghostly sounds as they chase the other players. Each person they tag becomes a ghost who also has to mimic the sounds and arm motions of a ghost. The game is over when everybody is a ghost.

This game is so versatile. On Thanksgiving you can make everyone turkeys that run around catching everyone while clucking "gobble gobble." Or use your school mascot for another version of this game. During one seminar, which occurred on an election day, we creatively changed ghost to a game of presidents. Once tagged by a president, a player had to mock shake a

Ghost

potential voter's hand and make a campaign slogan, stating, "If elected I promise to ______." The laughter was tumultuous, and the campaign promises hysterical.

The Gift of the Game

Ghost is a great game to start every play session with. This accumulation tag game sets the tone for playing fair, using safety, and taking care of each other, and it involves all the players in an equitable way. Plus, you get to act real silly. If your children have difficulty holding hands, this is a great way to start practicing.

We've also found that most children want to be the starting ghosts in the middle of the circle. We announce that we only pick those who are being quiet and good listeners to be our starting ghosts. Wow! Instantly, the pleading stops and the waving arms relax. Suddenly it's hard to find only four good listeners. Children learn quickly that positive behaviors are rewarded and that there is a time for silliness and a time for being attentive. Their attentiveness is rewarded very quickly with their silliest ghostly shrieks and actions.

PEACE PATROL AND GREMLINS

(Second grade and up, ten to forty players, a basketball court with painted lines, no equipment)

How It's Played

This is a classic battle between the forces of the noble peace patrol and the mischievous gremlins. Play occurs on a basketball court with painted lines. Choose one gremlin for every six to eight players in the game, with a minimum of two gremlins and a maximum of five. Everyone else is a member of the peace patrol.

The object is for the gremlins to freeze the entire peace patrol by tagging all its members. The goal for the peace patrol is to rescue its members every time one of them is frozen. The game starts by having all the gremlins meet in the center of the basketball court and count down to zero. The peace patrol members will scatter themselves all over the rest of the playing area. To make the game much more challenging, *all* players (both gremlins and the peace patrol) must stay on the *painted lines* and can only move or run around when they are touching a painted line with at least one foot. After the game has begun, the gremlins spread out along the lines of the court and begin tagging and freezing members of the peace patrol. Once tagged by a gremlin, a peace patroller cannot move. To let other members of the peace patrol know he needs to be rescued, the frozen player waves his arm over his head and repeats, "Save me!" Unfrozen members of the peace patrol will hear his alarm and come to their frozen comrade's rescue. When rescued (gently tagged) by an unfrozen peace patrol member, the once-frozen peace patroller is free to run and save other frozen comrades.

Peace patrol and gremlins

If a gremlin misses stepping on a line while chasing a peace patroller, that gremlin must count out loud to twenty. During this counting process the gremlin loses her ability to freeze peace patrollers. However, when a peace patrol member misses stepping on a line, he also becomes frozen and must stay that way until rescued by another hero. Peace patrollers do not have to count to twenty when frozen but should be encouraged to call out, "Save me!" to be rescued. The painted lines are very important and provide a great opportunity for giving feedback about playing fair.

A round of peace patrol and gremlins typically lasts five to ten minutes. Multiple rounds should be played to allow all the children to experience saving their friends.

The Gift of the Game

Everyone in this game gets to experience what it feels like to be a knight in shining armor—or Superman, Wonder Woman, a policewoman, a firefighter, a parent, a nurse, a doctor, or most important, a good friend. To feel like a hero is to be the rescuer and receive all the gratitude while doing something helpful for another person who needs your assistance. These are wonderful feelings that most people, especially children, don't get enough of. Being helpful is incredibly empowering and nurtures a child's desire to be compassionate. Children learn that being helpful is what human beings do for each other. Learning how to give as well as how to receive becomes the cornerstone for healthy "relatedness" and wards off antisocial behaviors.

ARE YOU A PEACEBUILDER?

(Kindergarten and up, ten or more players, an inside space, stable chairs)

How It's Played

Players arrange their chairs in a circle with about one foot of space between chairs. One person is selected to be the first PeaceBuilder. This player does not have a chair and moves to the middle of the circle. The PeaceBuilder then selects one of the players sitting in a chair and greets him with a handshake and the phrase "Are you a PeaceBuilder?" The person in the chair must respond (in a very loud voice so everyone can hear), "Yes, I'm a PeaceBuilder, and I like people who ______." (At this point the sitting player uses his imagination to identify some attribute that several or all of the other players sitting in the circle might have. For example, he might specify people who are wearing something green, who are wearing shorts, who brushed their teeth today, or who like ice cream.) Now the action begins. All players possessing the given attribute must leave their current chair and find another place to sit, which was vacated by another person having this same attribute. Pushing or shoving are not proper behaviors for PeaceBuilders, so competition to find a chair cannot be rowdy. At the end of the chair changing, one person will be left without a chair, and this person becomes the next one to start a new round by asking the question,

"Are you a PeaceBuilder?"

We have developed a rule that players are allowed to be in the middle only once during the game. Children will often want to be the center of attention and will play in a way that lets them be the remaining player after chair exchanges. When this happens, have that child select another child to take his place.

Are you a PeaceBuilder?

The Gift of the Game

The positive association, affirmation, and actions of being a builder of peace are highlighted as students play this activity. It is essential that the children practice announcing that they are PeaceBuilders. This game publicly helps children state to their peers that the concept of being a PeaceBuilder is alive and well at their school. This activity includes everyone as equals and promotes opportunities to practice caring and sharing while they are involved in mild competition. This moderately active game is perfect for the leader to process positive behaviors in a contained setting. Everyone gets a chance to laugh, have fun, and live the good values that happen when peace is put into action.

Safety tip: To prevent shoving as children rush toward the same chair, enforce the following chair-tapping rule. Whoever taps the chair first, with her hand, is the player who gets to sit in the chair. This rule effectively diminishes aggressive behaviors, softens the game, and makes it even more enjoyable. Always use safe and sturdy chairs.

TROLL TREASURE

(Second grade and up, eight or more players, 30-by-30-foot outdoor or indoor space, a piece of "treasure," such as an empty plastic bottle or a field-marker cone)

How It's Played

Telling a story will set the tone for this game of fantasy, strategy, and sneakiness: There once was a huge troll, a snarly, grumpy type who liked to find treasures and keep them hidden away. The most valuable of all the treasures was the "beautiful pearl-white dish-soap bottle," which the troll stole from the museum. (When explaining the game, have the children say, "Ooohhh!" every time you say, "beautiful, pearl-white, dish-soap bottle.") Now, the beautiful pearl white dish-soap bottle ("Ooohhh!") was kept in the middle of the troll's hideout. (Place the bottle on some significant spot in the middle of your playing area. Using half of a basketball court works really well since there are nice boundary lines on four sides.) The citizens from the town found the troll's hideout and sent their bravest people to retrieve the beautiful pearl-white dish-soap bottle ("Ooohhh!") from the troll and return it to the museum.

At this point, line all the students up on one side of the basketball court. Randomly pick one student to be the first troll and have the troll stand guard over the treasure. From the beginning of the line, count off five people to be the first challengers to attempt to retrieve the treasure from the troll.

Now it's very important to know some facts about trolls. First of all, if they touch you, you turn into stone and can't move anymore. A second fact is that they can run around inside the boundary lines of their hideout, but they can't go past those lines. Third, they can't touch the treasure with their feet or hands, and they must stay standing up unless they are tagging someone.

The game begins by having the troll roar a ferocious warning to the first five treasure hunters. Upon hearing the roar, they enter the boundary area and circle around the troll from all angles, each trying to snatch the beautiful pearl-white soap-dish bottle ("Ooohhh!") from the middle of the playing area. Every time the troll touches one of the players, the player becomes immobilized (turned to stone), and a new player is sent in from the line. If someone takes the treasure but is tagged before he gets past the boundary line, he also is turned to stone on that spot. The troll returns the treasure to the middle of the playing area. The treasure hunters cannot kick or pass the treasure to anyone else. Eventually, one of the good citizens grabs the treasure and races outside the boundary line. This person becomes the next troll, and players who were on the court become unfrozen. They go to the end of the line, and a new game begins. Like our other games, which foster sharing, you can only be the troll once. If you do swipe the treasure again, you get to choose someone who has done something nice that day to take your place.

The Gift of the Game

This is a wonderful game to help children practice playing fair. They must acknowledge if they were frozen and learn to settle minor disagreements. With practice, they will develop strategies of sacrificing themselves to get caught at critical positions, which will block the troll from tagging someone else, thus assisting the successful retrieval of the treasure. The structure of the game also teaches children patience as they wait their turns in line. Even the beginning of the game, when the troll roars, gives children the chance to practice being silly and taking healthy risks. They enjoy returning stolen treasure to its rightful owner.

Universally, this game is a playground and neighborhood favorite. Children and teens will play this one for a long time. We know monitors at many schools who start their recess with troll treasure for their first graders and continue the same game, in the same location, as each grade comes and leaves the playground. Empty *plastic* dish detergent and soda containers make good treasures. (Ooohhh!)

COSMIC MOTIONS

(Third grade and up, although modifications can be made for younger children, eight to thirty players, inside or outside space, several Nerf balls and other objects—*be creative*)

How It's Played

After the big bang, all the stars, planets, and comets wandered the universe without purpose. Finally, they have come to your playground, where you can put the cosmos into its proper motion.

Have the participants form a circle and raise one hand. You now must establish the orbits (pattern) of the objects that you have in your universe. The leader calls out the name of a player with her hand up and gently tosses her a star (a yellow Nerf ball). Having a hand raised in the air just means that the student has not yet had the star tossed to her and is waiting her place in the orbits of celestial objects. Once someone's name has been called, the person is permitted to keep his hand down for the remainder of the game so he can easily catch balls tossed to him. (Hand raises are just used at the beginning of the game to establish a constant pattern of who will toss to whom.) That player who has received the star now calls out the name of another person's (someone who has his hand up) and throws the ball to him. Remind the children that they must always remember who they threw the ball to, because that is the person they will always throw to. Have the students continue throwing until everyone has caught the ball from someone. When the last person has had a chance to catch it, the leader raises her hand, and the ball is tossed to her, completing the orbit and allowing the tossing to begin again. Practice the order at least one more time, making sure all students throw to the same person they threw the ball to the first time. Remind them to always call out people's names before throwing to them.

Now you're ready to add a planet (a different colored Nerf ball). Start the star (the ball from the first round) going around the circle. After it makes four or five orbits, add the planet. If that is going well, add another planet. Now try something different by

Cosmic motions

adding a comet. The comet (often a Frisbee) gets handed *around* the circle from one player to another in a clockwise direction. Now add a moon. It gets passed around the circle in a counterclockwise direction.

Black hole! Take a brief pause from passing the star, planets, comet, and moon around the circle and identify your black hole (a distinctly different Nerf ball). The black hole gets passed in *reverse* order around the circle. Reverse order is when players toss the black hole *to* the person that they received all the other stars and planets *from*. Practice this reverse direction at least once to make sure everyone knows where to toss the black hole. Now put all the other objects back in motion.

Hint: It really helps to call out the name of and establish eye contact with the person to whom you are throwing the ball, so he is ready to catch it.

Special rule: If planets collide, don't worry, because your group belongs to a "no-fault universe." No child has to run into the center of the circle to retrieve his ball where he might be bombarded by a planet. (Remember, this is a game of cosmic motions and not dodgeball.) As the balls gently roll to any individuals in the circle, they'll pick them up and put them back in motion by throwing them to the person they normally throw to. When a wayward planet is accidentally tossed to the wrong person, just have that person place the planet back into orbit by tossing it to whomever they usually toss to. Try bouncing or rolling one or more of the objects.

Cosmic elimination is an advanced version of this game, in which a star, planet, or other space object gets eliminated if caught by a person having the black hole. During this phase the black hole can be passed to anyone in any order.

The Gift of the Game

Mastery over skills, especially seemingly difficult ones, such as juggling, is a sure way of increasing anyone's self-esteem. To perform this activity, cooperation must be nurtured and self-control maintained. If your group is able to juggle only one or two cosmic-motions items on the first attempt, consider that successful. The children will enjoy greater success each time they play this game.

But there is more that can be gleaned from this activity. Children can have their academics reinforced kinetically through cosmic motions by juggling the celestial bodies of the solar system, the names of presidents, the names of continents, and more. We even know of a massage school that has modified this activity to help its students remember origin and insertion of muscle groups.

SILENT BALL

(All grades, any number of players, one ball or more if desired, indoor or outdoor area. Obviously, a quiet activity)

How It's Played

Usually, we don't like elimination-type activities, but the values this game teaches make it such an overwhelmingly successful experience that we had to add it to the list. It helps students solve problems and learn patience and self-control. Begin by explaining all the rules clearly, and answer everyone's questions before you start.

Start with all the players standing in a circle. Have everyone count down: three, two, one, zero. Once you reach zero, *nobody* (teacher included) is allowed to talk at all—not a peep! Play begins by throwing the ball to any player you wish. If the throw was good and the catch was good, then play continues. There are three ways to have someone's role change from a ball tosser to a sitter. The first way is when the throw is inaccurate or too hard or when it involves some other factor that the group decides is a throwing error. Then the player making the throwing error must sit down where he was standing. The second way to change roles is when the person who was thrown the ball drops it. In this case, the player trying to catch the ball must sit down. The third way is that whenever players speak out loud, laugh, or make sounds, they must sit down. This even occurs when someone wants to ask a question or get a clarification. If you break the silence, you must sit down. Players who end up sitting down must remain silent and cannot catch the ball.

As expected, there are many times when a judgment by the group is required to indicate if the thrower or the catcher has made the error. A *silent* consensus process must be used to work out this problem. Some groups point elbows at the person they think made the blooper. Majority rules. Be creative with your judgment technique. Players who are now sitting are still eligible to participate in this part of the game as long as they remain silent.

Since this game does remove players from part of the action, it is very important to keep the play moving. Make throws and catches progressively faster or more challenging, so the children make more blunders. Add another ball, have them stand on one leg or catch with only one arm to make it even more difficult. We recommend playing until five or six players are left. Multiple winners create a greater positive reward for the group. Clarify any rules between games, and restart the activity with everyone. One possibility is that sitting players who talked can be briefly timed out from the next game to help them recognize their need to control their behavior and play fair. After the games are over, you might want to process any frustration the children experienced.

The Gift of the Game

For years, silent ball has been used by teachers as a diversionary activity on rainy days. But this game can be so much more. What has been exciting for us to see is the transformation in thinking when teachers realize that games are potential classroom management tools. The quiet, calming effect of silent ball can be used therapeutically at any time on any day. Teachers are now playing a single round of the game before reading or when the class returns from recess and the kids need to settle down and control their behavior. Instead of trying to bribe the class with "If you're good, we'll play a game," we now see teachers assessing the temperament of the class and using an activity like silent ball to quickly achieve those good behaviors. The struggle to gain control of the class has been replaced with fun, and the class can move forward to the next academic task.

DETECTIVES

(First grade and up, fifteen or more players, indoor or outside, no equipment)

How It's Played

Have your students make a circle and close their eyes. Quietly walk around the inside or outside of the circle and lightly tap a few players on the head to become freezers. (Generally, pick one freezer for every six to eight players). The others become detectives and can now open their eyes as they begin to quietly *walk* around the playing area. The object of the freezers is to sneakily touch the other players, thus freezing them. Once frozen, the children become statues and remain still until they are saved. When another detective gives them a warm hug, the freezing spell is broken. The object of the detectives is to figure out who *all* the freezers are. They can't shout out the name of a freezer, but it is smart to keep away from them.

Freezers are so sneaky that they can pretend to be frozen and quietly freeze you when you try to save them with a warm hug. If two freezers touch each other, nothing happens, and the freezers can deduce that they just met another freezer. After a couple of minutes, stop the game and have the freezers raise their hands, so the detectives can see how many freezers they identified. Play again, having each freezer pick one replacement by tapping someone on the shoulder while everyone except the former freezers has his eyes closed.

The Gift of the Game

Like silent ball, detectives is an excellent transition game that can gently wind children's energies down so they may return to the classroom ready for academics. We enjoyed discovering a tag game where the players walk rather than run. Excitement does not always mean speed and intensity. Joy and exploration of thoughtful, intuitive behaviors can happen at a relaxed pace. This is important for children to experience. Sometimes the world is clearer at a slower pace. People can observe more when they are attentive, curious, and calm. Again, we adore games where the object is to rescue the players and not eliminate them. And rescuing others through warm hugs teaches compassion and appropriate touching.

ENDANGERED SPECIES

(First grade and up, fifteen or more players, large playing area, identifying markers)

Endangered species

How It's Played

Use a large playing area, about the size of a basketball court. Have your class identify the name of an endangered species (such as a panda, whale, tiger, or condor) for the focus of the game. Let's pick pandas for this example. Choose two or three trappers, give them identifying markers (like bandannas or balls), and have them go to the middle of the playing field. The trappers' goal is to capture the pandas by gently tagging them with their hand. A captured panda has been caught in a net and can no longer run around. Luckily, the other pandas can work together in teams of two or more to free their trapped friends. Two uncaught pandas hold hands while encircling the captured panda. They now raise their arms up and down, yelling, "Panda free!" This breaks the spell of the trappers' net and allows the panda to roam free to save other caught pandas.

There are many strategies in this game for both the trappers and the pandas. The trappers can guard the captured pandas.

When the trappers look tired or when they capture all the pandas, the game ends. A new endangered species is chosen with new trappers, and the game begins again.

The Gift of the Game

This is one of the best activities we know to blend learning with fun and build a more cooperative school community. In most of the schools where we have worked, classes of similar grade levels do many learning projects together each year. To maximize the values taught in endangered species, try scheduling one of these cooperative projects for the week when you will be teaching your environmental curriculum. Have each class pick a different endangered species to study and make a large poster stating all the facts critical to this animal's survival. Share your posters with the school by placing them in the hallway, and plan a time to look at the other classes' posters. Simultaneously, during the week, play your class version of the game during your regular activity period.

Here's where the real fun happens. At the end of the week, meet with *all* the classes involved and play each class's version of the game (using pandas, condors, tigers, and other species). The gift comes from saving another individual during the game. This is obviously a very nice experience to share with your class. However, it is so much more significant when the students begin to practice these behaviors in their larger mixed-classroom communities. By interacting with many different classes, the connections are quickly made that saving everyone is important. All the classes need to work together for their mutual benefit. Playing and learning together can break down unnecessary barriers that occur between classes. This makes the total school environment more livable for everyone.

HILLBILLY TAG

(All grades, ten or more players, identifying markers, large playing space)

How It's Played

Set up boundaries. Choose several players to be it (one for every six to eight players with a minimum of two its), and give each of them an identifying marker. In this tag game you can choose to run around trying to avoid being tagged or to link up with another player to be safe. Linking up is done only in groups of two by interlocking arms at the elbow with the players facing in the *opposite* direction (the classic swing-your-partner square-dance move). When two players are linked up, they are safe from being tagged by one of the its. Since players who are linked up each have an available arm, a third person can join on one of the open sides. But when he does, the player on the opposite side must unlink. Players can also choose to unlink at any time.

The its try to tag players when they are not linked up. When a player is tagged, he becomes it, and the identifying marker is passed to him by the previous it. This game has lots of potential for creating new rules and again is an excellent source for giving positive praise to everyone.

The Gift of the Game

This is probably Snoopy's favorite game because it's like dancing. The simple action of the swing-your-partner moves makes everyone laugh and feel good. The real gift, however, comes from using this activity to promote safe physical contact between peers. Hillbilly tag is a step beyond hand holding and the logical step before hugging, which is done in safety haven and detectives. The fast-paced action of having multiple players who are it forces the remaining students to seek refuge with anyone who is close enough to link up. Again, in this game, children practice saving and helping each other, which is far more useful than elimination or intimidation.

Schools can use this activity to mix classes together without the negative effects of pitting one class against another competitively. When your goal is to make your whole school a peaceful community, you must put your words into concrete actions that the children can perform. Let their creative spirits soar while they dance and play tag.

BROKEN WHEEL

(Kindergarten and up, eight to thirty-six players, large open playing space, no equipment)

How It's Played

Here's a game in which you get to invent the wheel and then fix it every time it gets broken. Players sit on the ground in rows, one behind another, in groups of three to six (depending on the size of the group). The sitting groups are arranged so they resemble the spokes of a wheel. All of the players in the spokes will be facing the center of the wheel. Now you're ready to start the game.

Select one person to be the leader. This person starts by walking around the outside of the wheel and eventually taps the last person in the line of one of the spokes and says, "Broken wheel!" The person who was tapped and *all* the players in that particular spoke now follow the leader in a race around the outside of the wheel. The race ends when the players reach their original place and sit back down behind each other facing the center to reassemble the spoke. The last player to make it back becomes the next leader and will walk around and "break" another part of the wheel.

Once everyone has the basic race down pat, the time for innovation begins. The wheel breaker can call, "Broken wheel hop on one leg," "Skip," "Go the opposite way," "Walk backward," "Sing 'Row, Row, Row Your Boat,'" and so on. Monitor the activity well, so the people in the race don't collide or run through the middle of the wheel.

The Gift of the Game

Broken wheel has given us one of the funniest experiences we have ever had. Usually we teach this game to younger classes, because

Broken wheel

it is the next creative step beyond duck, duck, goose. However, on this day we were dealing with a particularly aggressive fifth-grade class that was dominated by boys wanting to play dodgeball. Dodgeball was not going to be fun for everyone, so we selected different games to allow everyone a safe time.

What a treat! The game had progressed from the simple phase of racing around and sitting down to the point where the leader can call out whatever option he wants. The five "cool" guys were all in one spoke of the wheel when this girl, thoughtfully and with premeditation, tapped the last boy on the head and said, "Broken wheel, cartwheels." With the precision of a gymnast she performed a dozen rapid cartwheels around the outside of the wheel and sat down. The five boys floundered like fish out of water as they somersaulted, rolled, and basically tumbled their way around the circle. It was hysterical, but it was clear to all that no one had made fun of them. During the compliments, the girl received numerous kudos for a skill that others now respected. The gift of play should allow everyone to shine.

MICROWAVE POPCORN

(Kindergarten and first grade, any number of players, indoors, imagination)

How It's Played

Have children sit on the floor on their bottoms. Start the game by pretending you are going to make popcorn. Have the children pretend to go to the pantry by opening an imaginary door and looking inside at what's there. One person might see a box of cereal. "That might taste good, but it's not what we're after," you say. Another might see a jar of peanut butter. "I like peanut butter, but we'll put that back for now." Finally, you spot the popcorn. You pick it up and pretend to put it in your microwave oven. Have everyone set the timer and push the start button. At this point, everyone becomes a kernel of popcorn ready to be cooked. Have them start by wiggling a little bit as they pretend to get warmer. Then wiggle faster. Wipe their foreheads because they're really getting hot. Fan off their brother and sister popcorn kernels. Begin to sizzle as they rock back and forth even faster. It's time to pop! Stand up and start jumping up and down while saying, "Pop, pop, pop!"

For even more fun, try making caramel popcorn by pretending to pour caramel over the popping corn, and when one person touches another, the two stick together by holding hands and so on until the whole class has made a giant caramel popcorn ball. After the game I always like to pretend to eat some of my microwave popcorn.

The Gift of the Game

This version of Terry Orlick's sticky popcorn is a delight for the players. In all imagination games everyone is equal. Imagination, or "pretend," games hone creativity and camaraderie. Pretending to retrieve items from the pantry or from a refrigerator keeps the kids attentive and focused.

Microwave popcorn is another creative game that aids in crowd control. Children need to learn how to become excited without hurting each other. When standing up and sitting down on the floor, many young children often step or sit on other children. They need to become aware of their physical space and boundaries. Learning how to "pop" together without hurting another child during the caramel pouring is valuable. You may want to model how to "stick," jump, and sit down together with one of the children prior to the game. Also, we encourage you to have the children successfully practice this skill before playing subsequent rounds of microwave popcorn.

ROLLING LOGS

(Kindergarten to second grade [older people like it too], two or more players, soft playing surface, no equipment)

How It's Played

This activity is based on Terry Orlick's log-roll game. Pair children up and have them lie on their backs on the ground. Their feet should touch each other so that they look like one long log. The idea is to roll over in unison, so their feet don't come apart. Now try two, three, four rolls. Change partners often and repeat log rolling. Next try touching hands and rolling. Ready to make it more fun? Try crossing legs or arms. Now make bigger and bigger giant redwoods by having two players touch at the feet and another player touch at the hands. Build the numbers up until the whole class is attached. Give lots of praise to the children working together.

The Gift of the Game

It was a wonderful spring day when I accompanied a third-grade class out to the field, intending to play deep-sea diver and giants, elves, and wizards. It was pleasantly quiet as we walked out in a nice, orderly line. All of a sudden, four or five kids sprinted forward and began rolling in the grass. Quickly the whole class followed, and so did I. Kids really respect you when you join them in what they are doing. We continued this unstructured fun for a good while, and then I changed my agenda and taught rolling logs with incredible success.

Excitement and boundless energy are part of children's lives. I felt blessed that I was able to suppress my adult urge to demand control and allow these students the freedom to express themselves in an unpredictable but appropriate manner. It also felt good to have developed a wide repertoire of activities over the years so that I could playfully restructure the children's energies into an enjoyable team-building experience.

PSYCHIC NUMBERS

(First grade and older, any number of kids, anywhere, no equipment)

How It's Played

Divide the students into groups of three or four. Have the group choose a psychic number from one to fourteen. (Let's say they picked nine.) Each player uses one hand and the group counts, "One, two, three." Upon saying, "three," each person displays from zero to five fingers. The group counts up the total number of fingers shown and sees if they totalled their psychic number. Once accomplished, they choose a new number. The group can use both hands and try for larger psychic numbers. Another version is for one player to secretly think of the psychic number and only tell the group whether their total is higher or lower than the desired amount. After three attempts using their fingers, players try to guess what the psychic number is.

The Gift of the Game

Teachers often request activities children can do in small groups. They also need short activities to help kids stop fidgeting behaviors when they're standing in lines or waiting between other activities. Psychic numbers is such an activity, and it reinforces addition, subtraction, and multiplication skills.

One principal showed us her lunch line of children who were all playing psychic numbers. She said, "Last week, before our school's Healthy Play training, our lunch line was disruptive with children hitting and teasing each other. Today, with minimal encouragement from our monitor to play psychic numbers, there is laughter and learning.

"When we first planned to use psychic numbers as a lesson, it took three times longer than we thought it would. At first, the students didn't understand how to make their numbers, and it seemed like a real mess. But after demonstrating by writing the numbers on the board, sure enough, someone in each group caught on. Things went like wildfire as the students took over and patiently explained how to play the game with each other."

Teachers often state, "We play psychic numbers almost every day. It's so great when students do the teaching and the learning, and it carries over to their other math work in class." Aren't the minds of human computers really amazing?

SLOW-MOTION TAG

(Kindergarten and early first grade, four or more kids, inside, no equipment)

How It's Played

Begin by having everyone sit close to each other on the floor. Ask all the children to move their hands in slow motion. Now begin picking things that can be tagged by the students in slow motion. The leader will say, "Slow-motion tag people's feet." Students gently tag only feet that are within reach. Players must always keep their bottoms on the floor, glued to the place where they are sitting. Sometimes they won't be able to reach people far away. When they have completed the first tag, move on to another slow-motion command. "Slow-motion tag people's elbows," or "Slow-motion gently tag people's ears." (This one always makes me giggle.) "Slow-motion tag things people are wearing that are green or red or blue." You can tag their buttons, their hair, their socks, and so on. This is a great place to begin positive safe touching before the students play any other tag games. Gentle tags create more friends than aggressive ones.

The Gift of the Game

Many a primary teacher has told us, "It's my whole year's kindergarten curriculum! It's all the tools of multiple intelligence learning in one game: auditory, visual, tactile, interpersonal, intrapersonal, and everything else. I just can't get over it! We'll practice shapes, colors, body parts, personal boundaries, motor skills, just everything! It's also much easier to teach young children how to tag gently than to reeducate aggressive tagging tendencies." It is exciting to see discovery occur at every age and to acknowledge that prevention is easier than intervention.

SPOONS

(All ages, six to ten players per deck of cards, indoors at tables or on the floor, playing cards, some spoons or similar safe objects)

Hint: many games with cards do not need to have complete decks. If you've caught the feeling of why we play (to have fun!), then it doesn't matter if you're missing some cards. The game will still feel fair to everyone, and you won't have to compulsively count decks all the time. This also saves on expenses.

How It's Played

Up to ten players seat themselves in a circle or oblong shape. Spoons are placed in the middle and spread out so that everyone can reach them equally. There will be one or two fewer spoons than the number of people playing the game. Three cards are dealt to every player, and the remainder of the deck(s) stay with the

Spoons

dealer. After everyone has been dealt his cards, all players may look at their cards. The object of the game is to get three of a kind—that is, three kings, three sixes, three twos, and so on. Play begins with the dealer looking as rapidly as possible, one by one, at the cards remaining in the deck. If the dealer wants a new card from that deck, he or she just keeps it and discards another card from his or her hand, placing it facedown in front of the next player. If the dealer doesn't want the card, it is passed face down to the next player. (Each person can only hold three cards in his hand at a time.) Successive players look at the cards now being passed around the table, one at a time, and decide whether to keep them or pass them on. Eventually, someone will get three of a kind. At this point, they have permission to take the first spoon. This should be done as sneakily as possible, because if any other player sees a spoon being removed, she can quickly grab one, too. Once one player with three of a kind takes a spoon, then everyone else is allowed to take a spoon, regardless of the cards they hold. Eventually, all the spoons are taken, and one or more players are left without spoons. (We suggest having two or more spoons missing, as it shares the impact of not getting a spoon among multiple players.) These people are given an imaginary letter from the group, beginning with the letter S. If they eventually collect enough letters to spell out "spoon-sized-frosted-fruity-shredded-total-miniwheats," they are eliminated from the game. (If this ever does happen, you've probably been enjoying this game far too much for any one day.)

The Gift of the Game

This is one of the all-time great social games. It focuses on taking turns, being patient, being hurried, being confused, developing strategies to get the people with the fewest letters, and laughing. It offers a lot of room to make special rules. A favorite incident of mine occurred when two players simultaneously grabbed the same spoon and hung on tightly. With their hands in midair above the table, one of the other players wondered aloud who was going to get stuck with the letter. Without a moment's hesitation this girl (who will probably become a very successful lawyer) said, "Oh, he gets the letter. I'm holding the spoon part, and he's only holding the handle." Even he couldn't question this logic and accepted his letter without further argument. This is what we love about using a variety of games, which highlight different people's talents.

OVER, UNDER, AND AROUND KICK BALL

(Third grade and older, six or more players, large outside playing space, a soft Nerf soccer ball)

How It's Played

There may not be a better game invented for total teamwork than this one. Begin by setting up a long, straight boundary line. Divide students into two teams using the double-divide method (see page 62). Have one team scatter themselves across the playing field. The other team will form a straight line about three feet back from and parallel to the boundary line. The first person in line gets to kick first, and that player's original partner (from the double divide), who is now on the other team, gets to be his personal pitcher. After the pitch, the kicker may kick the ball anywhere *in front* of the boundary line. At this point, the real action starts.

The team in the field (the whole team) scurries over to the location where the ball was kicked. The objective is to form a line and have the first person in line pass the ball over his head to the next player, who passes it under his legs to the third, who passes it over her head, then under, and so forth, until everyone on the team has touched the ball in this sequential pattern. Any errors in the over-under sequence must be corrected before the ball gets passed any farther. When the last player receives the ball, the team in the field yells, "Stop."

While all this commotion is happening in the outfield, the kicker is busy trying to score runs by running circles around her team of players, who are standing in line. (The first few times you play this game you might find a few players running off in a traditional kick-ball manner around nonexistent bases. Use a gentle sense of humor as you remind them that they are to run around their team and not bases.) The at-bat team chants the score each time the player finishes running around the whole team. When the other team yells, "Stop," the player running around her team is finished and goes to the end of the line. The next player is now up, and their double-divide partner is the new pitcher. In over, under, and around kick ball there are no outs of any kind. Balls kicked behind the boundary line are simply replayed. An inning is over when everyone has had a chance to kick. Teams then switch places, and partners pitch to the player who pitched to them.

We've generally found it best to begin by keeping only individual scores. If your class can handle team score keeping, then you can add up everyone's runs or use the single-digit scoring method.

The Gift of the Game

We were playing seven-base kick ball (see page 118) with a group of fifth graders one day when a typical problem came up. Three players on one team kept hogging the ball and all the plays. Several kids started to look disgruntled, so we brought the game to a halt, sat down, and talked. Quickly, several students said they didn't like being left out of the game. Aaahhh, the game wasn't fun. We had come to one of the golden rules of play and decided to see if we could make things better. The class processed the difficulties and frustrations and made a rule that you couldn't run more than four steps with the ball before you had to throw it to someone else. This worked well, and the teacher praised them for solving their problem. Although they had learned something important, the teacher knew her class needed to practice more teamwork-oriented skills. She suggested that the following day they would try another kick-ball game: over, under, and around kick ball.

The next day they did, and it solved all those feelings of being left out of the action. The kids bubbled as they shared praise for their newfound teamwork and strategies. Each child felt a part of the game. They also made connections between the new game and the way in which they had tried to improve the game they played the day before. They were excited knowing that they had two great new kick-ball games.

NINETY-NINE

(Players who can add numbers to ninety-nine, two to eight people per group, inside, deck(s) of cards)

How It's Played

Ninety-nine uses all the wonderful social skills of other card games, plus it's great practice for addition and memory skills. The object of this game is to force other players to play a card that makes the score go over 99 points. Each player wants to avoid playing a card that will push the score over 99 and end the game. Before starting the game, make sure everyone is aware of the following special card values:

Ninety-nine

Aces: 1 or 11 points
Threes: Hold the score
Fours: Reverses the direction of play and holds the score
Nines: 99 points, no matter when they are played
Tens: Minus 10 points (–10)
All picture cards: 10 points
All other cards (2, 5, 6, 7, 8): Their face value

The dealer gives each player three cards, and the players wait until the dealing is done before looking at their cards. The first player to the left of the dealer starts and plays any card. This now starts the score, which begins at zero. For example, if a king is played, the score would be 10. This player must remember to immediately pick up a replacement card from the deck before the next player starts his turn, or she must play with only two cards. The next player plays a 7 and says the new score, 17, then draws a replacement card. The next person plays an ace and announces the score is 28. (Remember, an ace is 1 or 11 points, so the score could have been 18 or 28.) The next player plays a 9, and the score automatically goes to 99. (Remember, nines are special, and you don't add just 9 to the score.) Here is where the game becomes interesting. Unless the next person has a 3, 4, 9, or 10 in his hand, the score will go past 99, and the round will end. The following player plays a 10, which is equal to minus 10 points, so the score goes back to 89. The next card played is a 6, so the score is 95. Now, a 3 is played, and the score *holds* at 95. Another 9 makes the score 99 again. A 4 is played, reversing the play to the right and keeping the score at 99. Next, another 3 keeps the score at 99, and this is followed by a 4, which reverses direction again and keeps the score at 99. Finally, the next player does not have a 3, 4, 9, or 10 and forces the score past 99, thus ending the round.

At this point you can shuffle and start a new round, or to play down anyone losing, you might just keep going this way:

Let's imagine that the score was 99, and you are supposed to play the next card. However, you do not have a card that will keep you from going over 99. In fact, your lowest value card is a 5, which would make the score 104. Using the rules of creative play, if you place a card making the value greater than 99, you are allowed to subtract 100 from that value. So 104 minus 100 is 4. The score now stands at 4, and the game continues without shuffling or undue attention placed on the person who went over 99.

The Gift of the Game

This is a great chance to make math fun. It is important to allow all the players to add their own scores out loud, so that the fastest person in addition won't dominate the game. Every ten seconds, a player is validated by the group for properly adding their score. Players get more math practice by learning how to correct each other in a caring manner if an error is made. Obviously, you will not allow statements like "Hey, stupid, 33 plus 6 is 39 and not 41." Many students need practice in remembering details. Those with this difficulty will often find themselves with only one or two cards. (Maybe, if they practice remembering details in a game, they can transfer this skill to remembering to do some homework.) For many students, just practicing announcing the score may be the part of the activity that helps them progress in learning to speak up in class. It's never the score that counts. It's what you learn that matters.

LOW SCORE

(Children who are learning or who know fractions, two to six players per group, inside, decks of cards)

How It's Played

Developing a stronger memory is a special learning factor in this social, card game. The following cards have special values:

Ace: 1 point
Joker: 0 points
King, queen, jack: ½ point
Two through 10: Their face value

The object of the game is to get the low score with four cards. The dealer deals four cards, facedown, to each player. Players *cannot* look at their cards. When all the students have received their cards, each player may now look at only *two* of them. This is the only free chance a player gets to look at those *two* cards. From now on, they must remember what their cards are without looking at them again. (They do not get to see their *other* two cards at this time.) Players can develop any pattern of placing their four cards facedown on the table to help them remember which cards they want to keep and which they hope to trade away. Now play begins. The remainder of the deck is placed in the middle of the players, and the top card is turned over, starting a discard pile. The person to the left of the dealer goes first and may either choose the top card from the discard pile, which he can see, or take the top card from the deck, which he can't see. Example: Player X knows that two of the cards in his hand are a queen worth ½ point and a 7, which is not very good. The top discard is a 5, which really isn't very good either but better than the 7. The player ignores the 5 and chooses the unknown card from the deck. He now looks at this card and decides if he wants to keep it. He picked an ace, which is only worth 1 point, and chooses to keep it. This player can replace the 7 with the ace, or he can risk keeping both the 7 and the ace and discarding one of the two unknown cards. (He can look at it before he discards it.) He chooses to replace the 7 and now must remember where he puts the ace because he can't look at his cards again. The 7 is now placed on the discard pile and play continues. The following turn he draws another ace. He now chooses to replace an unknown card, which turns out to be a jack. Oops, too bad. This jack is now a discard, which the next player thankfully accepts. Play continues until one person believes she has the lowest total score. At this point she'll say, "Low score." All players now have to turn over all four of their cards and add up their scores for the hand. If the player who called low score is the lowest, she receives the bonus of not having to add any score to their accumulative game total. However, if any of the other players beats or ties the score of the person who called low score, she not only gets her point total for the hand but must add a 10-point penalty to their score. All other players add the point total of their current hand to their overall score. If the cards run out and players stop taking the top discard, then the hand comes to an end, and all the players total their scores without either the bonus or the penalty.

To practice the most math possible during this game, have every player keep a score sheet on every other player. Make the game more complicated by making jacks equal ¼ point, queens equal ⅓ point, and kings equal ½ point.

The Gift of the Game

Aaahhh, fractions! Those demons of math that defy easy computation. This is a great activity to let students practice working with these numbers and mathematical concepts. First, whenever you are playing a game where a written score is kept, have every player keep everyone's score tally. The point is to keep all of the kids active during the whole game instead of sticking one player with score keeping. Second, this game really lends itself to rule changes. The original setup of card values is easy. Once the children master those number skills, start changing values, for example have kings equal ¾, queens equal ½, jacks equal ¼—or kings equal ½, queens equal ⅓, jacks equal ⅙ point. You can even say fives are worth minus 5 points. Now you'll be adding and subtracting. The wonderful thing is that students can share and help each other out with adding fractions.

RANDOM NUMBERS

(Second grade and older, any number of players, indoors, a deck of cards *without the tens, kings, queens, or jacks*)

How It's Played

Students are each given four cards, and the leader selects two. Each card represents a digit in a two-digit number. Aces are equal to 1. For example, one player receives a 1, 3, 5, and 9. The leader, either a student or the teacher, has a 7 and a 4. The leader chooses the random number of 74. (You could have chosen 47 instead.) The player must now arrange her cards face up in any order to make two, two-digit numbers. The player adds these numbers together to come as close as possible to the random number. The first player could make 95 plus 31 for a total of 126. Not very close. Try 59 plus 31. That's 90, which is better. Try 19 plus 35, which totals 54. That's too low. Finally try 59 plus 13. This places her close, at 72.

Every student tries to come as close as possible to the leader's random number and is allowed to check her answer with her peers. Redeal the cards and select a new target number. Once the addition of random numbers is mastered, you can play the same game doing subtraction. Math is fun.

The Gift of the Game

One of the more exciting things for us is to return to a school where teachers have been using creative-play dynamics and find that the teachers want to teach us new activities that they have discovered or created. Random numbers was one such game. It's especially satisfying to see many teachers feeling so empowered that they search for useful academic games and then share them with their faculty peers. This exchange of games also adds wonderful spontaneity to our trainings while we and our participants gain new knowledge, which we can then pass on to others. To paraphrase some ideas from Arlo Guthrie, "Can you imagine hundreds of teachers playing games with their students every day? Why, they might think it's a movement." And, that's just what it is. Everyone has something to share.

NUMBERED CUBES

(Students who can work with whole numbers up to 5,000, two to six players per group, played at a table or on the floor, six number cubes [dice] for each group)

How It's Played

This popular game has been invented and changed by so many people it must be fun. It is a game for practicing when to keep the bird in the hand and when to try for two in the bush. Here is one set of rules to get you going, but we're sure you'll add plenty of your own personal touches to make the game better. The object of the game is to score over 5,000 points.

Scoring values:

Ones: 100 points
Fives: 50 points
Single twos, threes, fours, and sixes: 0 points
Three of a kind: 100 × the number on the dice

Four of a kind:150 × the number on the dice
Five of a kind: 200 × the number on the dice
Six of a kind: 500 × the number on the dice
1, 2, 3, 4, 5, 6 on the first roll: 1,000 points
All six dice scoring: 250-point bonus, plus the player's turn continues (if he or she wishes)

The first player rolls all six dice and looks for scoring combinations. For example, two twos, one three, one five, and two sixes were rolled. The only score for this roll is the single five. It is worth 50 points. The player may end her turn or set the five to the side and reroll the other five dice. She rolls again and gets three threes, a five, and a six. The three threes are worth 300 points, and the five is worth 50. This roll she has 350 points, which she adds to the first-turn subtotal of 50 for a total of 400 points. She may end her turn and score the 400 points or risk these 400 points by rolling the one remaining die (the six). She can only score on the single die by rolling a one or five. *Failure to score will cost her all her points for that turn.* Let's say she rolls and gets a one. This is worth another 100 points, plus she earns a bonus of 250 points for scoring all her dice. Now she has a total of 750 points, and she may continue by rolling all six dice again. She does and gets four twos, a three, and a six. The four twos are worth 300 points and the three and six are worth nothing. The total is now 1,050 for the turn. She can quit or go on. She rolls the two dice and gets two twos. This does not score. She may *not* combine them with the previous twos she has rolled. Therefore, her score for all this effort is zero. She took too many risks. It is now the next player's turn and so on. Eventually a player will accumulate several turns' worth of points and pass the 5,000 mark.

The Gift of the Game

This game features plenty of math and lots of social interaction: taking turns, taking risks, practicing how to make decisions, and listening to others offer a lot of advice about what they would do if they were you. Again, make sure that every player keeps every other player's score.

One rule we've left out on purpose is how to end the game fairly when someone reaches 5,000 points. Should the game stop immediately? Should everyone else get one more turn after the score is reached? Maybe those people who haven't had the same number of turns still get their last chance. There are many possible answers, and it is a good idea to have the kids develop their own fair solution.

BITE THE BAG

(Any age, two or more players, indoors, one tall paper bag for each group of six players)

How It's Played

The name of the game says it all. All you have to do is bite the bag. Ooohhh, gross! The object of this game is to stand on one foot, bend over, bite a grocery bag, and pick it up off the ground. Allow players as many chances as they want. Failure is frequent, but innovation is incredible as people contort themselves into bizarre poses as they try to defeat the bag. Once everyone has tried to bite the bag, the next step is to rip about three inches off the bag and start the process again. Keep making the bag shorter and shorter until no one can pick it up.

Hints: The reason we suggest so many bags is so that players do not have to bite an area where someone else has bitten. Also, as the bag gets shorter, you may want to station yourself as a spotter to help overenthusiastic players from nose-diving into the ground. Always remind players that the bag is worth about a penny, but the dental work if they crash on the ground is likely to cost hundreds of dollars.

The Gift of the Game

One of the things that we like most about this game is that it favors shorter and more flexible people. The overwhelming lesson from such a funny game is to reveal that all games are this silly. Basketball, baseball, football are really no more important than bite the bag. We are constantly amazed at the ingenuity of players who try their hardest to move on to the next lower level. This is another game where players can make up as many rules as they want. It's their game.

THE WALKMAN OF THE '50s

(Any age, two or more players, inside, an oven rack, a piece of string)

How It's Played

Take a five-foot piece of string and tie each end to one side of the oven rack. The first student winds the string around each of his index fingers so that the rack hangs about eighteen inches from his hands. Then he places his fingers in his ears. He bends over from the waist, so the oven rack is not touching his body. Then have the other participants gently strike the oven rack with any type of object they can find (car keys, pens, shoes, books, bracelets, soft-drink cans, whatever). Each object will produce a wonderful sound that will vibrate up the string to the listener's ears. What the "musicians" hear and what the person plugged in hears create two very different experiences. End your symphony with a gong: one person strikes the oven rack simultaneously with the heels of both fists, creating a deep and resonating note.

Hints: You can have little children wind the string, holding a full-size oven rack, around their *whole* hand and put their hands over their ears. Also, you could substitute a lighter metal object, such as a toaster-oven rack.

The Gift of the Game

If you ever attend one of our Healthy Play workshops, you will probably start off with this game. It's one of our favorites. It helps everyone start seeing that games really can just be for fun. If you can accept the risk of bending over with an oven rack plugged into your ears, then you are ready for anything. We encourage you to use this activity early on as you teach children the vast possibilities of having fun. If you are an educator, you might also use this activity to discuss the science of sound waves.

RUMPLESTILTSKIN

(Kindergarten and up, ten or more players, indoors, no equipment)

How It's Played

Ask participants to stand in a circle. Next select the challengers and have them move inside the circle. A good balance is to have one challenger for every six people in your group. This should allow for a dizzying pace of activity.

Instruct everyone to say the word *Rumplestiltskin*. Have everyone repeat it again as fast as they can. (Speed is important.) Next, explain the commands *left*, *center*, and *right* to all the participants. The significance of these commands is that the players who make up the circle must now learn the names of the other players on their immediate left and right and, of course, remember their own name, which will correspond with the command *center*.

At the same time, individual challengers from the middle will approach any member of the circle and give *one* of the commands (*left, center, or right*) followed quickly by "Rumplestiltskin." The player being approached needs to respond with the correct first name (based on the command given by the challenger) before the challenger finishes saying "Rumplestiltskin." If the challenger finishes saying "Rumplestiltskin" first or if the player being questioned gives the wrong name, then the challenger trades places with the other person and joins the circle. The other player now becomes a new challenger. If the person being challenged states the right name first, then the challenger remains a challenger and must try to find someone else to baffle. Players are moved about all over the circle and very quickly learn the names of many of the participants. Name tags are helpful.

The Gift of the Game

There is nothing more simple or direct in promoting self-esteem than being recognized and called by one's own name. It is not uncommon for children not to know all the names of their peers in their own classroom even months after the beginning of the school year. If people in your class don't think it is important to learn a particular student's name, that student might find it difficult to validate her self-worth. Rumplestiltskin changes all of that. Done at the beginning of the year, this activity creates name recognition, infectious laughter, and natural mixing.

Creatively and academically, this game has other great values. Let's say you want to teach your children the names of the original thirteen colonies, for example. Instead of having tags with individuals' names, have ones with the names of the colonies. You can repeat the names of the colonies on the tags as needed. Make sure that all the kids have one. Kids now have to say the name written on the tag to their left, center, or right. As they naturally are sent around the room, alternating between being a challenger or joining the circle, they begin to visually, linguistically, and kinetically reinforce their learning.

PENGUIN WALK

(Kindergarten and first grade, any number, indoors and/or outdoors, no equipment)

How It's Played

Young children adore this simple follow-the-leader activity. Have the children form a line with one child directly behind another. Inform the kids that we are all going to become penguins and go for a walk. Choose one child to demonstrate to the others how a penguin looks. That children will role-play the classic penguin look and movement: Arms held stiffly at their sides with hands pointed out at ninety-degree angles. The movement is a slow, gentle waddle. Also, point out that penguins make no sounds. You now find yourself in possession of a controlled line of happy penguin children that you can quietly take anywhere.

The Gift of the Game

Accompanied by our good friend Yosi Prince from the Ministry of Education in Israel, we arrived for our initial visit to a first-grade class at Lynn-Urquedes Elementary School. We were greeted by the teacher, who said that her class couldn't stay in line together without yelling, touching, or hitting each other, let alone play outside without aggressively invading each other's boundaries. Yosi had seen us in action implementing our activities with various classes but was curious how we would be able to address a class that couldn't even form a manageable line. Setting up the class for the penguin walk turned the process of lining up into an act of enjoyment instead of intimidation. Having to keep their hands by their sides and off each other and having to keep their mouths closed created a playful atmosphere. The teacher praised the class for their new ability to form and walk in a line. The children, even at this young age, experienced a successful group activity with little redirection from the adults. This spirit of cooperation carried over to more challenging games, which also were successful.

Hint: If the children are quiet and in line but still want to bump into each other, just remind them that "Penguins just don't bump into each other." It is our experience that children want to be mindful penguins. We've gone to schools and seen multiple penguin lines, and it is such a joy to see the children enjoying even the most mundane experience of walking through a hallway quietly.

FOX IN THE MORNING, FOX AT NIGHT

(Kindergarten and older, ten or more players, large open playing space, boundary markers)

How It's Played

The class is asked to stand shoulder to shoulder on one of the wider boundary lines of a large playing field, which becomes the forest. Choose one to four children to be foxes and ask them to go to the middle of the forest. Tell the children on the boundary line they are bunny rabbits who want to go to the other side of the forest where a delicious carrot patch awaits them. But before they can cross from one side of the forest to the other, the bunnies must first ask the permission of the foxes. They do this by chanting in unison, "Fox in the morning, fox at night, may we run with all our might?" The foxes have to respond with, "Yes, you may and yes, you might. And if you run, it will be all right!" The chase is on! The bunnies must run to the other side of the forest without being gently tagged by a fox. Reaching the other side of the forest without being tagged means safety and imaginary carrots. However, bunnies that were tagged are automatically turned into immovable bunny traps. They aid the foxes by reaching out from their immovable places and attempt to tag remaining bunnies during subsequent rounds as the bunnies run to the opposite side of the forest after chanting and receiving permission from the foxes. The round is played until three or four bunnies are left. They become the foxes for the next round.

We encourage you to change the dynamics of the game once it is successfully underway to keep it stimulating and to make it interesting for children who have other skills besides being able to run fast. Allow the foxes to huddle before the chanting begins and decide how they and the bunnies are to move through the forest. Instead of running, they could choose to have the whole class jump, skip, walk backward, or sing as they move from one side to the other. They will cue the bunnies on how everyone must move by changing their part of the chant and filling the desired action in the blank: "Yes, you may and yes, you might. And if you ______ , it will be all right!"

The Gift of the Game

Many school monitors have used fox in the morning successfully during recess when there are large numbers of children of multiple ages and few adults to monitor them. No doubt that with a larger number of players, manageability becomes more of an issue. But there will come a time when the school is ready to share the individual classroom successes of creative-play activities with multiple classes or even whole schools. This game lends itself to being played with larger numbers. Also, if the mode of movement is changed creatively and often, many children of all abilities can play without boredom setting in quickly. The chanting or singing brings the children the beauty, fun, sense of inclusion, and power to be found in singing. We need to help set the foundation for the upcoming generations to join in unison with their own "Give Peace a Chance" or "We Are the World" chants and songs.

FRIENDSHIP FREEZE

(Kindergarten through second grade, any number of players, indoor or outdoor space with room for the players, no equipment)

How It's Played

Popular in the primary grades, this activity helps make everyone feel special, and it provides a safe way to learn and practice appropriate touching. Children are asked to form the famous Creative Spirit "clump" by standing *loosely* together while still a group. You instruct the group that whoever can answer yes to your questions or statements is to raise his hand. The children who do not answer yes must find a child with his hand raised and gently hug him. Once they are hugging a friend, they remain frozen in that hug until the next question is asked. You should allow two children, one who is willing to hug and another who will be comfortable being hugged, to demonstrate to the whole class what a healthy, friendly hug looks like. The questions or comments should celebrate the ordinary things about being a human being, such as: "Raise your hand if you have an older sister. Raise your hand if you did your homework last night" or have a puppy, or like vegetables, or have smiled today, and so on.

The Gift of the Game

This game works on multiple levels. Young people need to learn what appropriate touching looks and feels like. They must learn that there is a vast and wonderful area of touching between erotic and violent touch, both of which are too often presented by the media as the only types of touching in our society. This activity is a wonderful tool for teaching those lessons. With this game, children find themselves easily mixing with their classmates while learning all the things they share in common. They can celebrate being special in being ordinary. Teachers may choose, from time to time, to highlight situations that may make some children feel different or uncomfortable. This can help them to get beyond feeling stigmatized. For instance, you might ask children who have a stepparent to raise their hands and receive hugs. Often they see they are not the only ones with this family dynamic, and they get rewarded for just being who they are. Remember we cannot give just lip service to the statement "People are what is most important." We must show that we celebrate all people for all that they are.

WHO'S IN CHARGE?

(Second grade and up, ten or more players, indoors is fine, imagination is the only equipment needed)

Who's in charge?

How It's Played

Ever wonder who's in charge? In this game students will have a chance to find out. Have your group sit on the floor or in chairs in a large circle. Select one member randomly and have him move into the middle of the circle. The person in the middle now closes his eyes while you, the teacher, *silently* point out one person (and only one person) to be in charge. The person in charge is the leader of the group, and all group members must copy exactly what this player does. While the person in the middle still has his eyes closed, the player in charge starts the game by making some type of motion, such as waving. Quickly, all the other members start waving. Now the person in the middle opens his eyes and begins to try to figure out who's in charge.

At any given moment the leader can change motions, for example, from waving to patting his head. Quickly, other group members see the change and copy the new motion. Now the person in charge (a silly person indeed) stops patting his head and sticks his tongue out. Everyone follows along. The person in the middle gets three guesses to try to figure out who the leader is. If the guess is correct, the two players exchange places and the game begins again. If after three guesses the person in charge has not been discovered, the game is halted and the great baffling leader is acknowledged. The person in the middle and the leader still exchange places and the game starts over. Encourage the person in charge to be very creative and use movements like clapping, shuffling feet, snapping fingers, making funny faces, moving in slooooww motion.

Hints: To facilitate sharing, players can only be the leader once each time you play who's in charge. It is also very important that the members of the group not stare constantly at the person in charge. Have everyone look all around the circle constantly. When you first teach this activity, try to pick players who have the imagination and the confidence to initiate changes during the game. This game can be played again and again, and over time everyone will get to show his skills of being in charge!

The Gift of the Game

Compared to adults, children have very little power in their lives. In most classroom settings there is an established pecking order where some kids have power and others have none. The beauty behind this game is the sense of empowerment children experience when they are the leaders and everyone follows their direction. Even children who cannot identify the leader are not humiliated and left in the center of the circle. And, as a discovered or undiscovered leader, this child then steps into the center to try to figure out the new leader. This makes all the players just participants, not winners or losers. We also have had many teachers tell us that this game really breaks up cliques. Children who often sit together are quickly shuffled around the circle. Often the boys sit on one side of the circle and the girls on the other at the beginning of the game. Since the person who was the leader must eventually give up her seat to the person in the middle, the children naturally end up mixing and so learn physical and emotional tolerance toward others. This game also breaks down the cootie factor.

GUESS WHAT WE ARE

(Primary grades, four or more players, inside or outdoor playing field, cones or dividers)

How It's Played

Divide the class into two teams, and place the teams on opposite sides of a playing area. One team jointly agrees on an animal, a person, or a thing that they want to be. They will soon present their new role to the other team. Once a decision has been made, the whole team must move toward the other team, playacting the thing that they have chosen. The other team shouts out loud what they think the opposing team is. When the players meet, the second team greets the first with an identifying handshake or pat. Teams switch roles for the next round. For example, team A decides that they want to be lions, so they crawl on all fours while mimicking roars. Team B shouts out their guesses, and when team A finally reaches team B at the dividing line, they extend their hands and greet the lions of team A, "Hello, Mr. [or Ms.] Lion. Glad to meet you." Team B now must choose an animal, a person, or a thing and present it to team A.

The Gift of the Game

The game of guess what we are provides hours of enjoyment when we play it with young children. We've also found that it is especially effective in classes where children have multiple challenges (handicaps). For children with limited cognitive and verbal skills or limited mobility, many games can be difficult. This advanced version of Terry Orlick's delightful unknown animals gives challenged children a game that meets their needs to have fun and be accepted. All children, regardless of ability, can either imitate or identify puppies, kittens, snakes, thunder, waterfalls, and more at their own communication level. This activity is also a fun way to mobilize fine and larger muscle control, and it can be worked into a physical-therapy routine.

GIANTS, ELVES, AND WIZARDS

(Third grade and older, the more players the better, large space, boundary markers)

How It's Played

Set up a playing field that is approximately forty feet across with an imaginary line down the middle and end-zone lines, which mark the safety zones. Have the players do a double divide to pick two teams. The object of the game is for one team to capture players from the opposing team, enabling captured players to now play for the "other" side.

There are three options in giants, elves, and wizards, and it is important to do group demonstrations of the correct positions. Giants stand tall with their arms stretched toward the sky. Elves crouch down and put their hands on the sides of their head to make big pointy ears. Wizards stand straight and wave their arms as if they were casting a magic spell. Each of these figures has certain powers and certain weaknesses. Giants beat elves. The elves beat the wizards. Wizards beat giants. It's a grandiose form of rock, paper, scissors. Every choice beats something, but every choice also loses to something.

The teams separate and hold a meeting where they vote on which of the three options the *whole team* will be. We encourage the thumbs-up voting format. Majority rules. Even when it is clear which role will be chosen, continue the voting process so that everyone feels that his decision matters. Once the voting is over, everyone on the team will act out the chosen role. After the huddle, the teams meet on the center line, face each other, and then take one step back so that there is some space between them. All players count out loud, "one, two, three," and then act like the character their team chose. Let's say team X chose to be giants, and team Y picked elves. Remember, giants beat elves. This means that team X will chase team Y and try to tag Y players before they can retreat to the safety zone behind their end line. All Y players who get tagged become members of team X. However, reaching your safety zone without being tagged makes you safe. If team X had chosen giants and team Y wizards, then team Y would chase team X, because wizards beat giants.

At the end of this round, newly formed teams regroup and pick a new character for their team. The game can be played again and again. If both teams choose the same option, all the players are instructed to laugh, return to their huddle, and pick again.

The Gift of the Game

Giants, elves, and wizards, one of our favorite New Games Foundation activities, offers many important lessons as well as a ton of excitement and laughter. In many games, children bicker over which team they get placed on. Some children feel threatened if they are not placed on the same team with their best buddy, or they become angry and resistant if they feel they are placed on the team they think will lose. The beauty behind this game is that though kids start out on one team, they quickly end up on the other. That's the point. During the after-play processing, children often say they played just as hard and tried their best on whatever team they played on. Lessons of tolerance, diversity, and trying one's best instantly surface and can be explored. We also use this game to defuse kids' ideas that they need gangs. Children and teens that successfully buy into giants, elves, and wizards learn that they can and should count on *all* their peers, no matter which side they find themselves on.

Modifying Favorite Traditional Games

SEVEN-BASE BASE KICK BALL

(First grade and up, fifteen to thirty-four players, outdoors, a Nerf soccer ball, seven identifying markers for bases)

How It's Played

The first alteration we suggest for traditional kick ball is to eliminate the three-out rule for each inning. This rule places too much pressure on one child to succeed or face her teammates' anger for ruining their chance to have fun. A more equitable inning is based on letting every player have a turn to kick. This could mean a team might make nine outs in a row and the other team might make nine home runs without making any outs. Once everyone on a team has had one turn to kick, their inning is over. What's really important is letting all the players get a chance to play in each inning.

The second variation is to expand the number of bases. Five, six, seven or more bases make the game much more exciting. And you can place them anywhere. You can even try making them unequal distances from each other. Another variation allows the runners to go either way around the bases. Players coming from opposite directions could both be safe on the same base. Maybe your class would prefer that players running in opposite directions can't be on the same base. Try both. The next change might be to eliminate foul balls. They are boring and slow down the fun. Besides, it's easier to get on base if the player can kick the ball anywhere. Backward kicks toward the backstop are a good way to get on base.

Some groups let players throw the ball at the base runners to put them out. A good, safe modification of this rule is to disallow any out where the throw is too hard. We also don't allow students to throw balls at a player's head or below the knees. Throwing at players' feet can make them trip and fall. Heads are vulnerable, too, so we don't count tags that hit a player's head. Safety is always paramount. Only use Nerf or other soft balls. Keep teaching that people come first in all games.

The Gift of the Game

For older students this is *the* game that will break down the barriers and let everyone play and have fun. Their eyes will be focused intently and their mouths wide open as you shatter the written-in-stone notion that there is only one way to play kick ball. You've got to lead this discussion of rule changes to believe it! And once the doors of innovative and creative play have been opened, your class will never play the same again. This game is a must.

Seven-base kick ball also lets children realize that no one wants to be the target of a hard rubberized ball thrown aggressively. Children quickly come to appreciate the kid-friendly nature of softer spongelike balls. In fact, at some schools where we taught enthusiastic students seven-base kick ball, they wisely opted not to play it again until the school provided softer equipment. Once the softer balls were provided, teachers reported that the children played this game frequently. Children really don't want to get hurt.

BASKETBALL

(Third grade and older, four to sixteen players, basketball court)

How It's Played

We've found that those children who love basketball will practice dribbling, shooting, and other skills as often as they can. Other children become increasingly removed from this game if they aren't so committed. Often adults or their peers don't give them a chance to practice or play. A great way to get kids to share the ball is to have a bonus of fifty points if *everyone* on the team scores a basket. Soon everyone on the team will be included, and the players will develop strategies to help that person who needs ten shots to make a basket. As a consequence, this person will get better. What excitement when the team cashes in on the fifty-point bonus!

Another idea that fosters teamwork is having all players on a team take a shot before anyone else on that team can shoot a second time. This continues for the second shot, the third shot, and throughout the game. Here are some other scoring ideas. Every player on the team must touch the ball before a shot can count. Try giving points for just hitting the backboard, allowing a double score if the ball rolls around the hoop and comes out. Add your own creative changes. Another possibility is to deemphasize the dribbling rule. Encourage those who can dribble to do so. Encourage the rest of the class not to worry if some players carry the ball occasionally or all the time.

The Gift of the Game

My men's group was celebrating a member's birthday with a picnic in the park and a game of basketball. One man brought his female significant other. Two of the men brought their young daughters. Now, my men's group is composed of your typical sensitive new-age guys, in touch with their own and others' feelings. But put a basketball in their hands, and some revert back to their traditional male conditioning. You know: Score at all costs, and competition is the name of the game. Just as in elementary school, the teams were divided into the boys versus the girls. To even out the teams, the girls' team asked me to became an honorary girl. The average height on the girl's team was about 4 feet 11 inches. The boy's team average was about 6 feet 4 inches, and they were aggressive players. It seemed likely this game would exclude or patronize the young girls. I quickly proposed that before a basket could count, the ball had to be passed and touched by all members of the team. My buddies, who were afraid of losing membership in the new-age sensitive-guys club, agreed with this idea. Automatically, the younger girls became equally important and necessary, and they were included in all plays when the girls' team got the ball. In fact, as an honorary girl (and certainly not the best-playing "girl" on my team), I also played more than I expected because of this inclusive rule. After the game, my male friends commented on how the game opened up for *all* the players and how much the youngest child's skills had improved. They saw that this benign rule change allowed that child to participate and practice and thus improve more than she would have in a traditional game of basketball. The guys still won that game, but we *all* left feeling satisfied, regardless of our gender, age, and size. We all felt exhausted but joyful at a chance to play and celebrate with our friends.

VENNIS

(Third grade or older, four to thirty-six players, a volleyball court with net)

How It's Played

One of our favorite volleyball adaptions is a game we call vennis. It's both volleyball and tennis with the major rule change being that the ball is allowed to bounce. Some groups like to allow only one bounce each time the ball comes over the net. Other groups allow one bounce between each hit. Begin by letting players practice while they learn to play more skillfully. Change the serving rules so players receive unlimited serves until they get the ball over the net. Let them serve closer to the net if that makes the game more successful and fun. Some players take a long time to learn this skill, so after three attempts, we let them throw the ball over the net. Another change is to allow more than three hits. At least once each game, every player on the team must volley the ball before hitting it over to the other team.

Scoring options can really change the game. Try playing for a cooperative score, wherein both teams try to reach a combined number of successful volleys back and forth across the net. Another idea is to score points based on the number of players who touch the ball (maximum of three) before they knock it over the net. Each time the ball comes back to your team, you must start over. In this game, either team can score, regardless of which team serves the ball. This last idea helps players focus on just playing and not getting hung up on the score. After both teams have served, have the serving players rotate to the other team. All of a sudden, fate can move you from the team that has the low score to the team that has the higher score. But watch out, because six rotations from now you'll be back on your original side. Have fun!

The Gift of the Game

My all-time favorite game of vennis was played with some children and teenagers in the psychiatric hospital where we both worked. It was during Christmas recess, which made hospital life even more difficult because these kids were not happily enjoying family, friends, gifts, and good food at home. At 10 A.M. we went out for the one-hour morning recreation period. One of the kids suggested that instead of allowing just one bounce between players, we should try two bounces. We also agreed to have an unlimited number of players hit the ball before knocking it over the net.

The first serve and subsequent volleying took almost three minutes to resolve the play. Players and teammates ran through the open gates of the fenced court to retrieve errant balls before they could hit twice. Balls hit over the net but out of bounds were chased down and carefully hit back to their side of the net, where they tried again. One volley must have lasted nearly ten minutes before the ball finally bounced three times. The game lasted two hours and forty-five minutes. We all gave up out of complete exhaustion and total satisfaction. The final score was 2 to 2.

THREE-BALL SOCCER

(First grade and older, the more players the better, at least three Nerf soccer balls, soccer field or large playing space)

How It's Played

Probably the best thing to do for soccer is to add more balls to the action. (Again, we recommend nice, soft sponge balls because they are so people-friendly.) Playing with three balls really increases the excitement, and if you use five, almost everyone scores a bunch of goals during the game. You'll actually have people trying to keep track of the score, but unless the game is videotaped, there is no accurate way to keep track.

Another useful addition is to have more than one goalie. Anytime a goalie gets tired of playing that position, he may choose

Three-ball soccer

anyone on his team to replace him. Usually, with multiple balls, people in the field get so tired they need a rest and will want to be a goalie.

The Gift of the Game

I had taught Mrs. Swanson's fifth-grade class three-ball soccer the week before, so this week I was planning to teach over, under, and around kick ball. To my pleasant surprise, the kids had used some of their class money to buy three Nerf soccer balls. When I arrived, the students could barely contain their excitement, as they had plotted to use their three balls and my three balls so we could play six-ball soccer. Even more enjoyable was when the teacher said to me, "Watch how *they've* decided to pick teams." She announced, "Find a partner who you think has similar soccer skills." Without manipulation or squabbling, the students quickly found appropriate partners. The class completed the double divide and had teams with amazingly equally skills. Kids know how to be honest about their abilities. They just don't want the consequences to be failure, humiliation, and loss of esteem.

An Important Recap

Here's a quick recap of the important concepts of *Learning to Play, Playing to Learn:*

Play is the most natural way for children to learn. Through their play activities, children often learn relatedness and socialization.

Learning how to use play therapeutically is easy. We first need to accept and embrace two essential principles. One principle is that we play to have fun. The other is that people are the most important part of any activity.

Then we must honor our two essential rules. First, if somebody becomes hurt or injured, whoever is closest to that person stays with that person until he or she is ready to rejoin the game. Second, it's okay to disagree or have an argument, but you have to do it outside the game and cannot come back into the game until you've come up with an appropriate peaceful solution.

After doing a few game activities, it is vital to immediately do a short processing session. This way you reinforce all of the positive behavior that the kids have accomplished during their activity time.

One must understand that there is a logical and practical continuum of game activities, starting off with "creative play." The central premise of creative play is that all games are just made-up notions. So you can change any game or rule to meet the needs of those people who are participating in the game.

One gentle final reminder: None of the games we advocate are worth hurting your body over. So, monitor yourself and your students or children. Monitor and model your personal readiness. If you or your students feel the need to sit out an activity, that's perfectly okay. When ready to join in, everyone should feel invited to do so.

With this as a foundation, we are ready to move on to "compassionate play," the next game type on our continuum.

Compassionate Play

It doesn't take a rocket scientist to notice that in Western culture, most game activities and sports seem designed for the highly skilled few who play to win by defeating others, often through intimidation.

The goal of *Learning to Play, Playing to Learn* is to help us all become advocates and active elders, so every participant can benefit from all the values identified on the "Why do we play?" and "What is the most important part of all games?" posters. Remember those posters? Children uniformly give the following answers to those key questions: They play to have fun, to make friends, and to feel good, silly, and accepted. The most important parts of all games are the people, as well as sharing, playing fair, and being safe. These are *all* worthy values. The only way to achieve these values is by fostering compassion among *all* the participants. The only way to forge compassion is through creating trust in oneself and others.

Trust exists on multiple levels, but it is clearly seen on two. There's the physical level, and then there's the emotional level. On the physical level, the issues are: "Can I trust myself not to put myself in any kind of situation where I am going to get hurt?" And "Can I trust all the other people I am playing with to respect my body?"

On the emotional level, we ask, "Can I trust myself and others to protect my self-concept?"

A little bit of personal sharing (Spencer talking). Years ago, I had a work-related injury that resulted in two herniated disks and a hypermobile sacrum. I was in a lot of pain and definitely limited in terms of my mobility. The first reaction I had was immediate withdrawal from almost any kind of physical activity because I was certain I was going to reinjure myself. And I was sure that everybody else on the planet was going to exacerbate my pain. What was even more devastating for me than this physical component of my pain was the emotional component. I was thirty-three years old at the time, and I was used to riding my bike about 12 miles a day, as well as working and playing daily with teenagers (and keeping up). Before my injury, my concept of self and my identity were those of a physically and emotionally healthy adult. Yet, all of a sudden, my self-concept was changed dramatically and my trust of self and others decreased exponentially. I was unable to join in physical activity until I could meet my trust needs.

I relate this story not because I want the reader's sympathy but to make the point that this fear of self and others, these issues of trust, are emotional baggage that I continue to bring to all game activities, even though this injury happened years ago. On some level, trust issues surrounding my physical and emotional pain remain to this day.

Children universally seem to bring trust issues to game areas. They think, "Gosh, I'm the last one to be picked. I'm not good enough. I feel too clumsy." As they feel these thoughts, they invent wonderful and/or not-so-wonderful defense mechanisms to avoid play. As they avoid, withdraw, isolate, or act out, they often bring trust-defeating baggage to their play spaces. As teenagers and adults, they will continue to bring trust-defeating baggage not only to their play activities but also to their work. We adults, having lived through these experiences and their consequences, know this all too well, don't we?

Total trust can never be achieved unless we address personal, emotional, and group social factors compassionately. Values like kindness, caring, sharing, being able to be silly, allowing for failure, tolerating and appreciating that failure, protecting everyone's self-concept, and eliminating teasing are so important. These are all vital ingredients to creating a trustworthy game and a safe environment for personal and group growth.

The Five Cs

The New Games Foundation came up with a wonderful formula that helps everyone identify whether a game that you are playing with your kids is a safe, successful and ultimately trustworthy. The formula is called the five Cs. A safe, trustworthy, successful game is one that's contained, cushioned, controlled, and played with a sense of caring and community.

1. A trustworthy game is *contained.*

   You know exactly where the boundaries are. You know exactly where you need to be to play the game. If you are not ready to play the game, you can move outside the boundaries, knowing that no one will humiliate, ridicule, or intimidate you for not playing. This freedom to decide when to take a healthy risk is an important one. We must encourage children to develop a sense of "personal readiness." When is it okay to join in an activity, and when is it smart to avoid participation? Personal readiness allows for increased awareness of oneself, others, and the immediate environment. Children will have many challenges placed in front of them throughout their lives. Let's help them practice making wise decisions. Giving and practicing choices will facilitate healthy risk-taking and learning to identify one's personal boundaries.

2. A trustworthy game is *cushioned.*

   Your activity is played on the most appropriate and safe space. Unfortunately, in our travels to multiple schools around the country, it is clear that most playground spaces contain glass, rocks, and other objects that are really dangerous to kids. During school off-hours, campuses often attract people who don't respect community property. We need to help the children and staff reclaim their campus. Additionally, we want them to reestablish that they are worthy of being safe and can take personal responsibility to see that this happens.

   Turn that responsibility into a game before playing any of your scheduled activities. Create an "eco-walk." Get all the kids to line up, shoulder to shoulder. Then instruct that they walk from one side of the playing field to the other, picking up all items that look unsafe. Then they deposit those items in a trash receptacle.

   In cushioning a game, we do whatever we can to make it a little bit safer. For instance, our local TV station reported that in the 1995 playing season, there were a reported 160,000 Little League injuries that resulted in trips to an emergency room. CNN reported that in 1993, there were more than 115,000 injuries in organized children's baseball leagues and four deaths. The deaths occurred when children were hit in the chest and went into cardiac arrest. Four deaths. Wow! So should we stop playing baseball? The answer is clearly no. Baseball is a great game when played safely. So how could we make this particular game a little more safe, a little more cushioned? Playing with effective yet softer balls might help. So might more protective gear and slide-away bases. And at least one adult present should be able to perform CPR.

We are not guaranteeing that by using the games outlined in this book you and your children will be free from injuries. No one could make that guarantee. Accidents happen. However, we can make a significant dent in injuries resulting from purposeful acts of aggression and violence by enacting the philosophy advocated in this book. As responsible elders who have been entrusted with the care of children, we must remain diligent in creating safer environments for them. Using foresight and common sense and correcting mistakes are ways that we can give activities greater safety, trustworthiness, and cushioning.

3. A trustworthy game is *controlled*.

   It is really important that we not be afraid to stop any activity that gets out of control. Our idea for educational systems is that we don't have to play any game for the full four quarters or just because there are twenty minutes left. We can stop any activity if necessary. We focus on key socializing aspects before we focus on scoring or winning.

   By permitting yourself to stop a game when acting out occurs, you give children an opportunity to explore what they need to do to bring the game back under control. Parents and teachers who stop unsafe activities really focus on improving social skills. If we let games go until the end of their allotted time, ignoring any acting out, we are missing the chance to really teach and learn through those activities. So not being afraid to halt games, bringing the kids together, listening to their solutions, and getting their input is valuable. If they can't offer solutions or are unable at that time to practice them, then it's time to move on to something else. Remember that with this concept comes the awareness that learning to play is all a process. No magic pills or immediate long-term solutions. You are going to try solving your game's problems today, and if it doesn't work out today, you'll come back to it tomorrow. You might find yourself saying something like "In three more days, let's try solving this problem and play this game again. It seems apparent that we're just not ready for it today. We've been unable to make this activity fun. And we must always play to have fun. So, let's try again in three days."

Additionally, take yourself out of the role of being the only one who is doing the problem solving. Don't fall into the trap of giving children the easy or obvious answer just because it is clear to your adult awareness. If you do this, then you will soon become a prisoner of children who come to you for all their answers. Let the kids participate and facilitate problem solving. You are in an excellent position to delegate responsibility to your children. This way, they can practice learning these skills in order to become healthier children and successful adults when they grow up.

4. Finally, a safe game, a trustworthy game, is one that is played with a sense of *caring* and *community.*

   Once again, we are trying to develop social skills. We are trying to bring people together at a very young age and teach them the skills that they are going to need to be successful children, adolescents, and adults. To do this, we need to create a compassionate and trusting environment.

We have a friend who is a therapist and when asked what she felt about therapy, her chosen profession, she said, "Therapy? I don't believe in therapy. What I believe in is caring communities, because if we had a real sense of community, of belonging, in areas where we lived, worked, and played, we'd probably need a lot less therapy. The greater a sense of community one feels as an accepted member, the less one will feel a need for therapy. If we really practiced true family values and created caring and nurturing communities, I could easily find myself out of a job. I would never just do therapy. I help create community."

The world can be repaired. But to do so, we must take action and engage wholeheartedly in acts of loving-kindness. And when we do, through compassion we create trust.

Although we have placed compassionate play second in the *Learning to Play, Playing to Learn* continuum of game activities, in many respects it embodies the first and most basic of the classifications. Compassion and trust concepts really begin for your class the moment you develop the two posters on "Why do we play?" and "What is the most important part of every game?" By doing this exercise, your class has empowered and trusted you (their elder) to help them achieve the values they have listed. It will be important for them to see that there is a serious personal accountability inherent to having fun during the school day. Your students must be able to trust and learn from your leadership.

In our seminars the initial activities we do are the most important of the whole training. These games must establish that trust and compassion will be actualized for every person attending. There will be no learning or enjoyment if these dynamics are not present.

We always begin by doing an activity called the Walkman of the '50s (see page 107). This game is clearly bizarre and therefore presents quite a personal challenge. It involves having a person wrap string around his fingers. The string is attached to an oven rack. The person puts his fingers in his ears and bends over slightly so that the oven rack doesn't touch his body. At this point, we call on the other participants to come forward and lightly hit the oven rack with their keys, pens, notebooks, coffee cups, and so on, to make wonderful sounds that only the person plugged into the oven rack gets to fully hear and appreciate.

What really is involved here is not just playing the activity but establishing trust. The first volunteer, who usually doesn't know us or any other participants, must take a personal risk by becoming the focal point of this activity. If we were to betray his willingness to try this activity, the training experience for everyone would be severely damaged. Fortunately, we take play very seriously. We never intentionally embarrass or humiliate anyone to get a cheap laugh. Respect is always acknowledged, and anyone can choose not to participate without repercussions. By successfully demonstrating this most awkward-looking activity, we show all the participants that their experiences during our seminar will be safe. A total trusting environment can often start with just one person.

The second game of our seminars is just as essential. Playing

Rumplestiltskin (see page 108) accomplishes the task of individual name recognition. There is nothing more important for membership in a group than having your identity known by the other group members. Yet we are frequently surprised that even in November, when the school year is well underway, many children cannot name everyone in their class. Trust and social development begin by having an identity.

Many trust programs do really exotic things. They have people balance on top of telephone poles with ropes, climb walls, and perform other daring feats. Creative Spirit does not advocate these experiences for the typical school setting. We believe children's trust development needs to be much more basic than this. We feel that before children are exposed to the high-wire act, they must first master simple things like appropriate touch and boundaries. In almost every class, there are students who have difficulty just holding hands. Kids also need to learn not to punch or push each other when standing in lines. Fierce name calling and put-downs are far too easily used by so many children. Before we can teach them exotic activities, we believe they need to practice giving truly meaningful praise to each other and tolerate simple tasks like holding hands or not pushing each other.

Practicing trust and compassionate behaviors will begin with implementing the caring-for-an-injured-student rule every time. Daily modeling will occur as the children use creative-play dynamics to develop safety rules that value people as the most important part of the game. There will be rules like hard tags or feet tags don't count. In kick ball or dodgeball, if someone is hit in the head with the Nerf ball, he is automatically safe. Additionally, the thrower of the ball must check him out to make sure he is okay. These simple behaviors develop compassion. Players who forget to do this need to sit out of the game for a brief time to remember what's important. This is the type of basic school curriculum that we have observed most children need to practice to facilitate a compassionate campus.

For trust to be present, it must be 100 percent. Anything less than that causes doubts. We realize that we are all human, but still, it is very important that we truly strive for this level of perfection.

Let's examine the concept of honesty and relate it to the educational grading process.

Pretend you are in an average class of fifth graders. Because it's a typical class, the kids often spend time gossiping about their teacher. One day you explain to them that you have decided to become an A-quality honest teacher. This sounds pretty grex. The best grade one could get in school is an A. Being an A-quality honest teacher certainly must be better than being a B-quality honest teacher.

So, from now on, we will grade honesty just like everything else at school. An A-quality honest teacher will tell the truth 90 percent of the time. To provide your students with their first trust exercise, you announce that you will now tell them ten personal facts about yourself. Nine of the facts will be true. One fact, and only one, will be a lie. This way you will be 90 percent honest. It will be the task of each member of the class to determine which statement is the lie. Here are my (Charlie's) ten facts:

1. I have lived in six decades.
2. My favorite color is bright yellow.
3. I usually don't match my socks and just put on whatever color of stripes I get.
4. My wife's nickname is Goldberry.
5. I was born in Buffalo, New York.
6. I went to Arizona State University to become a nurse.
7. I enjoy playing Rolling Stones songs on my guitar.
8. My pet dog's name is Hoover.
9. The name of my son is Forrest.
10. I enjoy playing chess.

At this point, the students can raise their hands and speculate which one of these facts is a lie. Someone always challenges my socks. But it's been over twenty years since I bothered to match them. Unmatched socks make sense. They make a more colorful pair. You don't ever waste time sorting them after doing the laundry. It's cost effective. When I get a hole in one sock, all the others still match it just fine. Next guess.

Usually people don't believe I call my wife Goldberry until I recite the several poems written by J.R.R. Tolkien about the wonderful woman of the woods who lived with Tom Bombadil. Quoting poems about your wife makes you a romantic. Not making her sort socks makes you easy to live with but weird.

Yes, we call our dog Hoover. She is really the best cordless wet or dry vacuum you could ever want. Drop some popcorn or spill some milk and all you do is call Hoover and it's quickly sucked up.

I was born in Buffalo in 1949 so that's six decades and eliminates those truths. I am a registered nurse who went to Arizona State University. An ideal afternoon would be to play chess with my son Forrest while wearing my favorite bright yellow T-shirt. That completes the nine truths.

The lie is that I play guitar. Only in my dreams did I ever play rock-and-roll guitar. I'm not even good at air guitar.

If you use this demonstration, don't give away the truth until everyone guesses what they think the lie is. The average group of students will challenge at least five or more things as being lies. If they are a typical gossipy group of kids, and even though you are a 90 percent honest teacher, they will question your credibility more than 50 percent of the time. Your 90 percent credibility now stands at 50 percent. So, ultimately, instead of viewing you as an A-quality honest person, they would now have to give you an F in honesty and trust you only that much. And they might never really be sure if they had figured out correctly whether you are lying or telling the truth. They might always wonder about every fact you tell them, even though you are honest nine out of ten times. The trust factor of honesty seems to erode exponentially when it is betrayed or hidden. Trust is also easier to lose than to gain.

Horseplay, like fake fighting, also erodes trust quickly. We try to point out that fake fighting often leads to real fighting and violence. "Oh, we're just goofing around" is the typical response from most children. To demonstrate our point we use the following example:

Pick a child and ask him if he can be serious with a demonstration. If he can, proceed. If not, find a child who can. Remember always to reward the other child for his honest response. State to the child you've picked, "Nine out of ten times, I'm going to come up to you and I'm going to give you a big smile and a nice handshake. Every time I see you, big smile, nine out of ten times. But, if I were to tell you that one of those ten times, I'm going to punch you in the teeth real hard, and it just might be this time, would you feel safe to shake my hand right now?"

An honest child will wisely state, "No, not at all. I couldn't trust you or your smiles. Odds are, you could hit me anytime."

Once again, that's how trust works. Trust can deteriorate quickly. A Russian-roulette version of trust will only set up an atmosphere of paranoia and fear. As much as humanly possible, we should keep trust as high as 100 percent.

Play gives you wonderful opportunities to practice 100 percent trust and compassion with your students. The great incentive in teaching social skills through play is that students want to play. They will modify their actions so they can be in the game.

When kids are lining up to go out to play and some are pushing each other, never hesitate to reflect that those using assaulting behaviors are not taking care of the people. Then have the offending students leave the line to have their disagreement. Once they've resolved their conflict, they can now join in at the end of the line.

If during rattlesnake tag (see page 151) certain girls or boys refuse to hold each other's hands, have them step out of the game until they can take the exact place where they started. Crushing someone's hand or pulling his arm is not being cute or funny. Children engaged in these kinds of actions are being aggressive. These little acts by children need to be immediately addressed. You will not be able to develop real trust as long as children are allowed to scapegoat their peers in front of others or the whole class. When their actions or words convey, "I'm not holding Skippy's hand because he's such a jerk," your leadership and quick intervention are necessary.

This concept of 100 percent trust is most effective when it is transferred to the whole school community. When you are walking on the school grounds give kids frequent praise for doing kind deeds. Regularly say things to the whole class like, "I want to thank Skippy for the way he settled his argument at lunch without fighting." Give your students incentive to gain your recognition for demonstrating positive values.

On the other hand, as you're passing down the hall and you see kids mock fighting, state, "Are you caring for the people?" This forces the children to briefly think about their actions. It is much more effective than saying, "Hey, break it up," or, "Hey, stop!" If a first grader falls on the way to the bus, the next kid shouldn't race over him to get the window seat. Bring that child back to do the caring, reminding him that he was closest to the injured child. Acknowledge behaviors that need challenging. All students must learn caring and shared responsibility for everyone throughout their campus. Caring and acting responsibly are not just the jobs of the elders.

Living trust behaviors is different from talking about them. It can change your class or the whole school. Children must practice compassion and problem resolution before they get older and think weapons will be an answer. How can gangs get started when everyone must care for everyone else? When you can count on everyone to take care of each other, there is no longer a need for protection. If you really want to minimize drug abuse, let kids practice taking healthy risks. Supply them with activities to fill their time meaningfully both during and after school. Compassionate play is very rewarding.

In this section of the play-dynamic continuum, we focus on activities that have strong trust and compassionate play elements to them. That doesn't mean that the other activities presented in this book don't focus on trust. Every game, as well as every action during the entire school day, has an effect on the trust level of the students, teachers, and parents at your school. What we want to do here is highlight specific resources you can use to help your students practice learning more about responsibility.

You will find a variety of trust games presented in this section. Pick the activities you believe your class is ready to try. Trust games have a natural progression that involves increasingly higher and more sophisticated levels of trusting behaviors. Not every class will do every one of these games. Some years, you may do more of these activities than others. Work with each class individually. It is important that you use your good judgment to choose the games that the children are ready to handle.

When we show our children that we see compassion and trust as key factors and that we care about each individual, they become able to take that trust and balance it with their own needs to feel safe, take risks, make changes in their lives, and grow.

Compassionate Activities

REMOTE CONTROL

(Fourth grade and up, two or more players, cones, either inside or outside)

How It's Played

This is a wonderful trust-building activity that allows everyone to be in power and under the power of the remote controller. First, establish a playing space (approximately 40 feet by 40 feet or larger) and find some obstacles—a row of cones, for example, or several chairs. Place them like barricades randomly in the playing field. If you're outside, the primary children's playground area where slides, swings, teeter boards, and monkey bars exist will work perfectly. Now place three destination markers (A, B, C) at strategic locations inside the playing area. Divide students into small teams of two to four people and have them establish a playing order. Space the teams around the perimeter of the playing field. The goal of remote control is to verbally guide your friends *safely* around the obstacles and to help them touch all three destination markers while they have their eyes closed.

Let's say you have twenty-four students and made six teams of four. Place the teams around the sides of the playing space and have the players count off to establish who will be the remote controller. Player 1 from each team steps inside the playing field and will be directed by player 2 (the remote controller) from outside the field boundary. The remote controller is allowed to walk around the perimeter of the field, close enough to be heard by the person with his eyes closed (player 1). Player 1 will search for and touch the markers in the order of A, B, C and then be guided back to the starting position. During this turn, players 3 and 4 will sit quietly and observe the action. As soon as player 1 finishes, player 2 will step inside, close his or her eyes and be directed by player 3, who becomes the remote controller. Players 1 and 4 will sit and watch. Player 2 will be directed in a different order, such as B, C ,A, before returning to the starting position. Afterward, player 3 will be directed through the course by player 4 and follow the order C, A, B. Lastly, player 4 will be controlled by player 1 in the order of A, C, B. As each team finishes, players are instructed to quietly sit and watch other teams complete their remote controlling.

The Gift of the Game

I remember when we made up this game. We were working with a group of fifth-grade peer mentors who assisted us with each of the younger grades when we went to play. It was the end of our project, and we asked them if they would like to do something special by being the first group to test a brand-new game. Excitement overflowed. The game was quickly organized, and chaos instantaneously developed. Our original concepts, not the ones outlined above, were way too complicated and confusing. The game was terrible. But, as with everything we do, we let the group fix the problems. *Voila!* A wonderful, sensitive, caring, and risk-taking adventure was soon created. Everyone liked being guided. Shy students had to practice yelling out commands so they could be heard. The group imposed the rule of quietly watching so "blind" players could easily hear. As expected, peers corrected each other and/or ceased inappropriate behaviors like walking someone directly into a barrier. Many practiced math skills as the remote controller, shouting out turns in directions in fractions and/or degrees to aid their "blind" friends. All the students congratulated each other on mastering the difficulty of giving clear instructions. Additionally, they talked, shared, and some even hugged. Now that's the way people can play in a trusting manner!

BLUE MAGIC

(Third grade and up, an audience, and one "telepathic" assistant)

How It's Played

After telling your student assistant the secret of how this game is done (see below), return to the classroom and give the following speech:

YOU: I was truly amazed when I came to your class today, for I felt magical and psychic energies flow between me and my assistant. [*Like a wizard, wave your fingers toward your assistant as you make your favorite science-fiction special-effects noises.*] And, to prove that there is a telepathic link [*once again making your noise*] between me and my assistant, we would like to demonstrate our ability to perform blue magic! [*Have your assistant close her eyes and then ask another student to point to any object or person in the room. Make sure all the children know and agree on the object or person that was picked.*] I will verbally call off random items in the room, but when I get to the correct one, even though my assistant's eyes were closed, through our telepathic link, she will be able to verify that it is indeed the item or person that was chosen. [*Now have your assistant open her eyes and let her enjoy answering no to all the incorrect questions and yes to the correct one, to the utter amazement of her classmates. Since you and your assistant know the simple secret, you will be confident that your assistant will guess correctly. Those who do not know the secret will be amused and awed.*]

Encourage the children to guess how the trick is done, complimenting them on their "excellent guesses" until the real answer is exposed. They will come up with a great number of possible solutions, from a numerical component to secretive hand gestures. It will seem like magic. Continue to do this activity, balancing the frustration tolerance with the enthusiasm of the class.

The secret: Tell your assistant to answer yes to the following question after an object which is the color blue has been identified.

Example: Say the class picked the clock while your assistant's eyes were closed.

YOU: Is it the door [*which is the color brown*]?
ASSISTANT: No.
YOU: Is it Veronica's shoes [*which are the color yellow*]?
ASSISTANT: No, of course not.
YOU: Is it Marco's jeans? [*The jeans happen to be blue and this is your assistant's clue. Your assistant will answer no to this inquiry, knowing that the very next item you name will be correct.*]
ASSISTANT: No, it is not Marco's jeans. I get no psychic vibrations.
YOU: Is it the clock?
ASSISTANT: Yes, of course it is!

Warning: You can play green magic, red magic, purple magic, or even plaid magic. But, unless you want angry parents to storm the office of your school's principal or district supervisor, *never* call this game black or white magic. These titles bring up and may promote images of occultism. Names of games are powerful, and you can sway an innocent activity in the wrong direction by giving it an inappropriate title.

The Gift of the Game

Nobody captures an audience like a magician. Someone who has mastered the seemingly impossible gets our attention. And this is important to remember when promoting ideas that break through resistance and complacency. The exciting thing about the activities that Creative Spirit promotes is their immediate marketability to the audience—in this case, children. Blue magic is a great bonding activity for your children who respond less to kinetic activities and more toward cognitive ones. This and other indoor activities help send the message that healthy-play values do occur inside the classroom as well as on the playground.

Experience has shown us that the greatest value comes from blue magic when youngsters take this logic puzzle home and play it with their families. Children report and experience a sense of satisfaction and excellence, and they feel special when they are able to stump their older siblings and parents. And they will. We were not able to solve the riddle behind blue magic right away when it was first presented to us. Family members who discover the secret have a chance to shower their children with praise for coming up with such a challenging and entertaining activity.

ACTION WORDS

(Third grade and up, any number of players, inside or outdoors, no equipment)

How It's Played

Select one player to think of a secret word. Then instruct this child, the leader, to announce to the group another word that rhymes with the secret word. For example: "My word sounds like *goat*." The group must attempt to guess the secret word. But to make a guess, they must put their guess into *action* by acting out their guess. One person might stand up and pretend to put on some clothes, miming the word *coat*. The leader will announce if *coat* is a correct guess. If not, another person might sit on the floor and begin moving her arms back and forth. "No, it's not a *boat*." A third person stands up and expands their cheeks and abdomen, and the leader states, "Yes, it's *bloat*." The child who guesses the correct answer is the new leader, and the game begins again.

The Gift of the Game

It is clear how this game can teach children about words that rhyme and even homonyms. What isn't as evident is how this activity honors and celebrates skills other than being the fastest and strongest. Everyone can play the simple roles for success in action words. We observed a teacher who used action words creatively to manage a child who often sought attention by disruptive imitation of others. She appropriately set limits on these behaviors and encouraged this child's natural acting skills in the appropriate arena of action words. The child got positive attention without putting others down. Another win-win situation.

PICNIC

(Fourth grade and older, the more players the better, inside or sitting down in the shade, no equipment)

How It's Played

Have players sit in a circle or around a table. Tell them that this is a logic-puzzle game. The goal is to figure out what items you can bring to get permission to go on a picnic. The players each take a turn and name an item they would like to bring on the picnic. For example: Charlie wants to bring chicken, and he gets to go. Tom wants to bring soda. He is told that this sounds delicious, but he doesn't get to go. Mary tries hamburgers, but she can't go either, even though hamburgers would be good to eat. Susan says she'll bring soda, and she gets to go. Why can Susan bring soda and Tom can't? That's the crux of this puzzle. The solution is that the players can only bring things that start with the first letter of their first names. Play logic-puzzle games in teams, so players can share answers and not feel alone if they can't solve the puzzle.

The Gift of the Game

When you first introduce logic puzzles to your class, you should begin with this game. The logical pattern in which children use their names to solve the puzzle is generally easy to figure out and sets the tone for the logic puzzles that will follow. You may want to help a child who needs a self-esteem boost by letting him in on the secret so he can be your assistant (or "ringer").

A TRIP TO WASHINGTON

(Fourth grade and up, four or more players, sitting down, no equipment)

How It's Played

The goal of this game is to figure out what to bring so you can get one of the ten seats on the plane for a trip to Washington. Players take turns announcing what they want to bring on their trip. Example: Bill might try to bring a *suitcase,* but he can't start the journey. Paula might try a *hair dryer,* but it's too early for her to go with that item. Tom might try his *wallet,* and he gets to start the trip and gets the first seat on the plane. Actually, anyone could have started the trip to Washington if he had brought a wallet or a watch or a Walkman. The key to this game is to bring objects starting with the letters that will spell *Washington* (wallet, alarm clock, suitcase, hair dryer, ice cream, and so on) *in order.* Next, try traveling to Paris or Egypt or anywhere else you want. It is useful to write the correct answers on the board so people can see the pattern.

The Gift of the Game

As you can imagine, this activity reinforces spelling as you have fun. Even when children solve the riddle to this my-rule game, they still want to play. So when you are teaching geography of the Middle East, play a trip to Egypt, Israel, Jordan, and so on. Young children especially like going home and stumping parents, older siblings, other relatives, and friends with logic puzzles once they know the solutions. It gives them a healthy sense of empowerment.

SILLY TILLY WILLY

(Fourth grade and up, four or more participants, inside or outside)

How It's Played

This is a favorite and quiet logic-puzzle game that will challenge students' spelling abilities. (It certainly challenges ours). The game starts by saying that you have a weird friend named Silly Tilly Willy. Now, Silly Tilly Willy only likes some things and really doesn't like others. The goal is to figure out what Silly Tilly Willy does and doesn't like.

Each player takes a turn saying, "Silly Tilly Willy likes ______, but doesn't like ______." The leader and those players who have solved the puzzle acknowledge whether another player has correctly stated Silly Tilly Willy's likes and dislikes. For example: Silly Tilly Willy likes to drive on the *street,* but doesn't like to drive on the *road.* She likes the *moon* and doesn't like the *sun.* Likes *trees* yet doesn't like *bushes.* Likes to *smell* things, but doesn't like *odors.* She's pretty weird! (The key to this puzzle is that Silly Tilly Willy only likes words with double letters and doesn't like words that don't have them.) The creative part of the game for the players in the know is to mislead others' logic by postulating items that seem to have some connection. A good example of this type of misleading connection would be that Silly Tilly Willy likes to gossip but doesn't like to tell secrets. Players in the know keep playing so they can both confuse and assist those players who haven't yet figured out the logic behind this puzzle. It is critical that people refrain from shouting out the answer when they solve this game.

Have players test their ideas by whispering to the leader what they think the correct solution is. Again, when playing logic puzzles it is useful to have teams and/or to write the answers on the board. We've known this game to go on long after everyone knows the solution just because the players are having so much fun coming up with tricky comparisons of Silly Tilly Willy's likes and dislikes.

The Gift of the Game

Boy, did we have to learn to spell better when we first introduced this game into our workshops.

These games really improve spelling and teach other lessons in grammar. For instance, eight-year-old Amber stumped and educated us all with her logic puzzle, a my-rule game, called "Guess what Amber likes," one day while we were in our car on the way to her friend's house. Her older sister Malia said, "Do you like dogs?"

"Nope," Amber answered.

Malia asked, "How about oranges?"

"No."

Older brother Jesse said, "How about our cat, Taz?"

"No, but I do like tomcats,"Amber said.

Mom asked, "How about catfish?"

"Yes, Mom, I like catfish."

Thinking I had discovered the secret to her logic I said, "You like things that have the word *cat* in them like *tomcat* and *catfish*."

"Good guess," said Amber, "but no."

The game continued. "Books?"

"No."

"Movies?"

"No."

"Newspapers?"

"Yes."

"Streets?"

"No."

"Roads?"

"No."

"Highways?"

"Yes, I like highways."

"Winter?"

"No."

"Spring?"

"No, again."

"How about summer?"

"No, I don't like summer, but I do like summertime."

Oh, we were stumped. If we had written down our queries and charted them against her yes and no responses, we might have been able to pick up Amber's secret rule to her logic puzzle. However, at the end of the game, in her most self-satisfied tone, she said, "If you'd review your guesses, it is quite clear that I like compound words. We learned compound words in school today." Bravo, Amber. The rest of us learned what compound words were in her mom's car.

If you want your children to learn how to spell the names of animals for biology, play "My pet alligator likes" as you might play Silly Tilly Willy.

ACTION/REACTION

(Kindergarten and up, two or any even number of players, inside, no equipment)

How It's Played

Pair up the players and have them stand about eighteen inches apart. Have the students face their partners with their arms held out toward their partner, elbows bent, palms touching their partner's hands. Have them slowly start the action by allowing their bodies to lean forward simultaneously. Then they increase physical pressure on their hands to break their forward momentum. Before they tire of holding one another up, start the reaction by gently pushing away from their partners until they are balanced standing up straight. As their trust grows, partners can move farther apart. After mastering two-people action/reaction, try groups of three or four. We do not advocate groups larger than four because the group becomes circular and the necessary tension for safely keeping balance is lost. In your class, you may want to have just a few students demonstrate this activity in front of the whole class, so you can be sure they are doing the action/reaction correctly. Remember, this is a game to build trust while having fun. Always highlight the message of safety and do not allow any aggressive pushing or teasing.

The Gift of the Game

We all know those famous trust activities such as "trust falls," "trust dives," and so on. These are great games but rarely appropriate for an elementary-school setting. They are just too dangerous, and people often get hurt. Action/reaction is safe and appropriate.

Trust activities often bring up anxiety. When we do this activity in our workshops, we often model the type of acting out and anxiety that games like this can produce. As I explain this activity with a volunteer from our group, Charlie begins to channel our friend Skippy and places himself on all fours behind our trusting volunteer, coaxing me to push the volunteer over his back for a laugh. We temporarily bring the game to a halt to let Skippy know that we will *not* hurt any of the people and that his behavior is not going to make him any friends. In fact, I usually ask the other players if any of them feel that they would want Skippy as their partner for this activity. The answer is a solid "No!" Kids act out for many reasons, from getting a laugh to playing out their fears. We must recognize this and help children learn which behaviors will earn them the trust of their peers, so that they can successfully make friends. Stopping an activity is a great way to let the children know that we, as adults and dependable elders, will act responsibly and help them discover healthier ways to act.

EMPATHY

(Third grade and older, at least twelve players, inside, no equipment)

How It's Played

We like to tell the story that the game of empathy comes from the wisdom of Native Americans who said, "The best way to know another human being is to walk a mile in his moccasins." Begin this activity by having all players remove their shoes and throw them into a pile in the middle of the floor. The leader begins circling the pile and comments on the unique wonders that the owner of each shoe has to offer. We suggest modeling by having you, the leader, first pick a shoe that would not be a comfortable choice to wear on your foot. (There is always some moderate anxiety in this game, and humorously picking a shoe that is too big or too little helps break the ice.) Now, find another shoe from a very different pair for your other foot and march around as you begin to experience what the original owners feel when they walk in these moccasins. Imagine what it must feel like to be the people whose shoes you are now wearing. Who are these people? Are they happy? Do you share common interests? What do you admire about them? Instruct everyone to find mismatched shoes for their feet, always being sure that a right shoe is on their right foot and a left shoe is on their left. Everyone now parades around and notices the fine choices all the players have made.

Now the tricky part. The goal, at this point, is to rematch the shoes while continuing to wear them. The leader finds someone wearing the mate of a shoe she is wearing and interlocks legs with this other person so that the shoes fit together as a pair, with the right shoe on the right and the left shoe on the left. All players follow the leader's example. Each player now has a shoe that is unmatched and must hold each other together as they precariously move around trying to connect with the other players to match both left and right shoes. The game ends when everyone has paired up both their shoes.

The Gift of the Game

This is not the first activity you want to play with your class, because students may feel it is high-risk or an uncomfortable invasion of their personal space. At the right time, however, this is one of the silliest bonding experiences that we know. Every group we have played this with has laughed and laughed while they hold on to each other and scuffle around to attach themselves to another person. The game of empathy breaks down barriers between people. We find out our similarities, such as everyone has warm and sometimes sweaty shoes. We also see that other people have different identities or tastes. They may like shoes that are fashionable, practical, or economical. The important thing about real empathy is that through genuine intimacy with others everyone gets to experience so much more in life, even fun.

RATTLESNAKE TAG

(Kindergarten and older, twenty to forty players, inside or outside, a rattle or shaker)

How It's Played

Begin by having everyone hold hands, in a circle. The people holding hands define the boundaries of the playing circle and become the safety net for this game. Their importance should be strongly emphasized. Now, randomly choose two players to play inside the circle. The two players in the middle decide which one of them gets the rattle. The object for the player without the rattle is to tag the person holding the rattle. But she must do so with her *eyes closed*. The player with the rattle keeps his *eyes open* but must constantly shake the rattle to let the other player know his approximate location. The person with the rattle tries to avoid being touched. The game begins with the two players standing far apart inside the circle. The player trying to catch the rattlesnake closes her eyes and spins around once or twice.

The safety net gently increases or decreases the size of the

Rattlesnake tag

playing field as the students move closer together or farther apart. One person will be chosen to be the safety-net monitor. This person will give various commands to the safety-net members. To help the person in the middle of the circle who has her eyes closed, the safety-net monitor may command the group to "take one giant step in" or "take three baby steps closer." This helps facilitate compassion for those players having a more difficult time tagging the rattlesnake while increasing the challenge for those who find this playful task easy. It's scary to move around with one's eyes closed, and many players may need to open them to check out where they are. This is a perfect opportunity to support safe play and deemphasize arguments about "cheating." Simply state that a player must acknowledge this by saying, "Oops," when she opens her eyes. When this happens, the game is temporarily halted until the person without the rattle closes her eyes again and spins around once.

The Gift of the Game

This is a great trust activity to start with because the inherent level of trust that this game requires is so very basic. Can the children hold hands, especially kids of the opposite sex? Can the person with her eyes closed trust that the safety net won't let go of their hands so that she ends up helplessly going beyond the boundaries and into a dangerous or humiliating situation? Can the person with her eyes closed open them due to discomfort or fear without being ridiculed as a cheater? Will she be able to count on the safety net to move in, making a tag easier? Can anyone in the class trust everyone for their emotional and physical safety?

This activity facilitates, highlights, and encourages trust behaviors. Children in the safety net are asked not to play unless they can hold hands firmly to protect the two in the middle. In fact, built into this game are immediate verbal rewards for children deemed most trustworthy by their peers. Each round, the person who will have her eyes closed selects the person she thinks is most trustworthy to be her own safety-net monitor. It is the safety-net monitor's job to assist and protect the person with her eyes closed. He protects her physical safety by stopping the activity when members of the safety net are not standing up or holding hands. He protects his buddy's self-esteem as he asks the safety net to keep taking baby or giant steps in, so a tag occurs before the child in the middle either loses face or becomes dizzy. To be picked the safety-net monitor or buddy is an honor, and most children feel proud to be thought trustworthy. To be trustworthy is a great attribute, yet many children are not often verbally or behaviorally rewarded and acknowledged for this essential quality.

Also, if you have a class where the boys and girls are quite separate and even hostile with each other, this activity quickly breaks down the gender barrier. Always announce that you want everyone to play, but the safety of the people in the middle is most important. Remind members of the safety net that they must hold hands to protect those in the middle even if it means holding the hands of a girl or boy. Start the activity with one boy and one girl in the middle. To enhance gender equity, when the tagging is done make sure that the boy and girl switch roles, so the tagger now becomes the rattlesnake. After each round, have the boy pick a girl and the girl pick a boy to replace them in the middle as they exchange their places in the circle for the next round. Before you know it, the circle is nicely mixed, joyous, and cooperative. Remember to instruct children to pick only those who are good listeners, who are well behaved, and who haven't yet had a turn.

Unless you have a lot of time, you will probably not be able to let all children take a turn in the middle. To facilitate giving everyone a chance and to shorten the time playing this activity, you might not want to have the middle children exchange roles before picking others to replace them. Or you might want this to be a game in which children learn delayed gratification. If so, you must acknowledge *before* the game that everyone may not get a turn in the middle this time. Perhaps at recess they will have their turn or maybe tomorrow when they play this game again.

Always stress the importance of everyone's role, including those trusting members of the safety net. Be sure to model and highlight compliments to members of the safety net for their faithful behaviors. We have had many parents and teachers report that this was the game that broke through that goofy boy-girl barrier. This is because everyone must hold everyone else's hand. There are no exceptions if students want to play. We've seen dozens of kids refuse to hold hands, and we've asked them to step out of the circle and watch the game. This is not punishment. This is just the safe expectation of appropriate behavior. By the second round of the game, they've conquered this acting out and have warmly joined the whole class. This intervention demonstrates how the constant practice that occurs during play can change the way your whole class will interact.

Finally, we like the way this game models sympathy for an individual's fears. Players are given permission to open their eyes when scared without fear of being labeled a cheater. You can almost feel the relief in your class when you, the elder, state, "It's scary to move with your eyes closed." Children may then learn to verbalize their fears and understand that others will help them. Modeling permission to be scared or uncomfortable is so important. This acceptance of normal human feelings and behavior allows children to practice honesty and personal responsibility. These are more valuable skills to practice than just chasing people with your eyes closed.

PERSONALITY

(Fifth grade up, groups of six to fifteen players, indoors, writing pad or chalkboard)

How It's Played

Players sit in a circle. One player is chosen as the leader for the first round. Another player is chosen to be the scribe who will keep track of questions and answers. The leader *silently* thinks of any one of the participants or of himself. The object for the participants is to guess the person the leader is thinking about. They do this by asking the leader *abstract* questions that will allow the leader to describe the *positive* essence or personality traits of the secret person.

The players each take a turn asking their questions as the scribe briefly writes down their question and the response. Questions should be phrased, "If this person were a ______, what type of ______ would they be?" Participants are encouraged to be creative with their questions. The questions should be broad in concept to give the leader many options for response. Example: "If this person were a *musical instrument* (or an *animal* or a *breakfast cereal* or a *country of the world*), what kind of muscial instrument would they be?" Note that these are not direct questions like "What color hair does the person have?"

The leader then must answer the question with a *positive* and *truthful* answer based on his own perception of that person's personality. After six to ten questions have been asked, the group reviews the data, and in turn each student makes a guess about the person the leader is thinking about. (It is critical that the leader *not* disclose the name of the secret person until *all* players have had their turn at guessing.) The scribe writes down the player's guesses and then tallies them, creating a record of guesses. The leader then discloses the identity of the person he was thinking of. Then the leader describes how each of his answers pertains to *positive* personality traits of the secret person. For example: "When you asked what kind of animal this person would be, I thought of an otter because Bill is always so playful and happy." After all the answers have been described, a new leader and scribe are chosen, and the game goes on.

The Gift of the Game

Kids can be the kings and queens of put-downs. Getting them to give or receive compliments is sometimes as difficult as nailing Jell-O to the wall. Personality answers this dilemma by helping kids give sideways compliments to others until they learn how to deliver them directly. Since this game takes some abstract thought, you probably can't play it with young children. Even some adults have a difficult time with abstract thought. Think fifth grade and up. Remind yourself and the children that you are going for questions and answers that describe what the leader thinks best represents or describes the person. This is not a game where you describe a person's favorite likes. For example, I was the leader who was secretly thinking of Charlie. Someone asked me, "If this person were a color, what color would they be?" Now I know Charlie's favorite color is bright yellow, but bright yellow didn't make me think of Charlie. Instead, I answered, "This person would be the color of the Arizona sunsets." Later in the game when I gave my reason for this answer, I said, "Charlie, who is so diverse, couldn't be just *one* color, he had to be many. And I see both the colors of the Arizona sunsets and Charlie as majestic and magnificent." Trust me, there was a bright smile on my buddy Charlie's face to hear himself described so positively and thoughtfully. This game works well with people's first impressions but shines when done repeatedly. Players grow in intimacy each time this game is played. On the children and adolescent wing of the psychiatric facility where we met, personality was the most popular game during our community meetings. Once the children and teens experienced the warm feelings of giving and receiving compliments and learning how positively others viewed them, they didn't want to stop playing this game. The outcome, answers, and comments were often so touching that we went through lots of Kleenex with all our happy tears.

Playing this game backward creates a game called reverse personality. Have your class write six personality questions on the chalkboard. Students then take a piece of paper and answer the questions about themselves. Have them sign their names to their papers, fold them up, and then collect them. Place the reverse-personality sheets of paper in a box for safekeeping. On days when you are between academics, need a pick-me-up or a two-minute filler activity, or are having one of those momentary brain cramps and don't know what to do next, just pull out a sheet or two of paper from your reverse-personality box and play a round or two. On picking a reverse-personality sheet, say, "This person thinks of themselves as a panda for the type of animal. The color is blue. When asked which cartoon character they'd be, they replied Cinderella. Type of food was Mexican. And when asked what kind of ice cream they would be, they said rocky road. Who do you think it is?" The kids tally up their guesses for the secret identity behind this round of reverse personality and then quickly afterward learn whose name was at the top of the sheet. The gift that many kids discover is greater insight about their peers while often realizing that many of them think alike and share the same qualities. They learn that their personalities are both similar and individualistic, that they are both part of the group and special individuals. You now have a box full of premade magic you can use all semester long.

Many teachers and principals have told us that our suggestion of opening every staff meeting with one round of personality sets a warm, validating, and productive tone for the meeting. The staff feels appreciated by each other, and group cohesion develops. This is so important because teachers, principals, and most school staff work autonomously. Remember, the creation of a caring community recognizes, supports, and encourages acts of loving-kindness.

COPY MACHINE

(All ages, groups of three players, indoors, no equipment)

How It's Played

Have players get into groups of three. In each group one person becomes the "original," the second is the "copy machine," and the third is the "blank page." We like to begin this activity by having students focus on using their hands. Instruct all the students to close their eyes. The originals form their hands and fingers into some peculiar shape. The copy machines must figure out the position of the originals' hands by feeling them. Finally, the copy machines find the hands of the blank pages and try to reform them to be just like the originals. The copy machines may talk to the players and are allowed to go back and forth between the originals and blank pages as often as necessary. When the final copy is finished, all players open their eyes to see how accurate a job the copy machine did. Everyone trades places until each player has been in all three roles.

As your students demonstrate the appropriate level of trust with each other, they can try more difficult copies using upper body parts, such as head and arms. For truly trustworthy groups of students, you may use whole bodies. You must make an appropriate assessment of your group's readiness. In making a complete body copy, the copy machines do their touching on the back side of the people being copied. In all trust activities it is important to set firm limits and cease any activity at the first sign of inappropriate words or behavior.

The Gift of the Game

In 1978 I was playing copy machine at a training for teachers, and our group included a woman who was blind. I assumed this was probably going to be a rather boring activity for her. I thought that the only fun and challenge in this game occurred after the copy machine had formed the blank page to look like the original and all the players *opened their eyes* to admire the success of the copy machine. How could this woman fully enjoy the game? She could never see the results. Oh, well, we went and played anyway. Almost all the other groups were finished, and the group with the blind woman still needed to let her have a turn as the copy machine. Everyone in the other groups was now watching these three people. I thought, "This could be very awkward."

Insight often occurs when you least expect it. What I thought might be an uncomfortable moment turned into probably the most successful activity of the day. This woman's hands danced with speed, agility, and comfort over the original's body. There were loud gasps of amazement from the onlookers as this woman rapidly and accurately transformed the blank page into an exact duplicate. She received an ovation from the group when she was done, and with a big smile she took a bow. At this moment I clearly saw that everyone really did have an equal capacity for enjoyment. In hundreds of occasions since then I have ignored my preconceptions and allowed the players to just have fun their way.

Cautionary note: Always use good judgment with this exercise and assess your participants before playing. Many groups never get around to playing copy machine because the group dynamics and/or issues of physical touch are so loaded that it is not advisable to play this game. If that is the case with your group, ignore this activity and enjoy the many others that are presented in this book. Always meet the needs of the individuals in your group to experience safety and trust. You have not failed if your group, or individuals within it, cannot tolerate copy machine.

LOST IDENTITY

(Fourth grade and older, the more players the better, inside, paper, tape, pen)

How It's Played

This is a great game for reviewing famous people students have studied in class. One person is selected to have the lost identity. Another player secretly writes the name of a famous person on the sheet of paper and tapes the paper to the back of the person with the identity crisis. Everyone in the group is now shown the lost identity as this player walks around the group.

The player with the lost identity must discover who she is only by asking yes-or-no questions of the whole group. (This can reinforce a great deal of learning about the famous person.) Let's pretend George Washington was chosen as the lost identity. Here are some possible questions and answers:

"Am I a man?"

"Yes."

"Am I a rock star?"

"No."

"Am I living?"

"No."

"Am I a scientist?"

"No."

"Am I an American?"

"Yes."

"Am I a president?"

"Yes."

"Am I Lincoln?"

"No."

"George Washington?"

"Yes!"

Pick another student and start the game again.

If at any point the person in the middle is feeling frustrated, she is allowed to protect her dignity and self-esteem by asking for a hint from the whole group. Hints should be designed so they don't totally give away the answer. The person who has the lost identity may ask for as many clues or hints she needs.

The Gift of the Game

One teacher we know shared an innovative way that she improved her children's test scores. On the day before her weekly quiz, she and her class played lost identity. Using historical and current-events figures learned that week, she reviewed their attributes, physical descriptions, accomplishments, and qualities with her class through this game. She saw improved scores the next quiz days because of this activity. Because the children wanted to be more successful at the weekly game, they spent more time doing homework and were generally more attentive in class.

SCISSORS

(Fifth grade and up, the more people the better, inside, a pair of plastic scissors)

How It's Played

This is another game that uses problem-solving skills with a game rule that the players must solve. The objective is to figure out how to pass and receive the scissors in a "crossed" or "uncrossed" manner. All players sit in a circle of chairs. The leader holds a pair of scissors, which she manipulates into one of many possible positions. For example: The leader says, "I have started with the scissors uncrossed, and I am passing them crossed." At this point she may turn the scissors upside down and open or close them with a look of intense concentration. The second person must say, "I have received the scissors crossed [or uncrossed], and, I am passing them crossed [or uncrossed]." The leader and all those who know the solution to this riddle will correct the player if he has made a mistake in how he says he has received or passed the scissors. Play continues to the next (probably bewildered) player, who tries to guess how he or she is receiving and then passing the scissors to the following person.

The scissors have nothing to do with solving this game. They are merely a diversion to what is really going on in the circle. The key to whether they are passing "crossed" or "uncrossed" is whether the player's *legs* are crossed or uncrossed. If players receive the scissors while their *legs* are crossed, this is what they must state. If while holding and manipulating the scissors in their hand, they subtly uncross their *legs,* then this is what they state about passing the scissors to the next person. Hint: Logic-puzzle games can be frustrating to some people. We suggest developing mini-teams of players based on the first three people sitting next to each other, then the next three, and so on. This way no single individual will be upset if he or she can't solve the puzzle alone.

The Gift of the Game

You know you are making an impact when your children take what they have learned and share it with others. After Thanksgiving, a fifth-grade girl related that she had played scissors with her family and all eighteen of their relatives. She let her seven-year-old brother in on the secret, and the two of them stumped the adults for over thirty minutes of fun and laughter. They felt empowered, respected, and enjoyed the positive attention from the relatives during this curious activity. This is the true positive social impact of play.

I DOUBT IT

(Fifth grade and up, groups of three to eight players, either at a table or on the floor, cards)

How It's Played

The goal of this game is to be the first player to successfully get rid of all her cards. Have a dealer deal all the cards out. It doesn't matter if some players get more than others. Play starts to the left of the dealer, and that person must declare how many aces he has and place them *facedown* on the table. He may have zero, one, two, three, four, or even more aces if you are using two decks of cards, but he *must* say he has at least one ace. Bluffing is an essential part of this game, because you must *always* put down at least one card. Players will often have to declare having at least one of something they don't really have. When a student has to make such a play, he simply substitutes one or more cards that are placed facedown on the table and declares his bluff. Players should try to be as convincing as possible so that people believe they are telling the truth about how many cards they are trying to play. If everyone believes a player's response, his cards are left on the table and play continues. The next player must state how many twos he is going to play.

During any turn, anyone may challenge the honesty of the player by saying, "I doubt it." At this point, the card(s) being played are turned over, so all players can see if the truth was being told. If the cards accurately reflect the face value and number of cards claimed, the player who doubted the other's honesty must pick up *all* the accumulated cards on the table. This can sometimes be a hefty pile. If the cards do not correctly match the claim, then the player not telling the truth must pick up all the cards. The sequence of play continues ace through king and then starts over with an ace until somebody finally gets rid of all his cards.

The Gift of the Game

It's great to have an appropriate place to put cheating. Have everyone acknowledge that this is one place and the only place where it's okay. You can use this effectively to redirect players in other activities where cheating is not part of the rules. We've played this game hundreds of times, and everyone has fun. As always, balance is the key to success. Players who try to cheat excessively get caught the most as their reputation catches up with them. This is a good lesson to show them that fact. We also like the way this game gives children practice in challenging statements they believe are false.

COOPERATIVE MUSICAL CHAIRS

(Any grade level, the more players the better, inside, sturdy chairs)

Cooperative musical chairs

How It's Played

We adore this variation on musical chairs, developed by Terry Orlick. Begin by telling the players that we are going to play musical chairs but in a new and improved manner. Since no one likes being eliminated in the traditional version of musical chairs, all the people in our version get to stay in the game, but the chairs still have to go. This means the game will have more people than chairs, and the people in chairs will have to share sitting down by letting others sit in their laps or on their knees. Model how to gently sit on the lap of another person. Also, demonstrate how people sitting in chairs can spread their legs to let multiple people sit on each knee. As more chairs disappear, more and more players end up sitting in people's laps or on their knees.

Have the group pick a song to sing and start marching around the chairs. Stop the song and have everyone sit down. Randomly pick some letters of the alphabet and have people whose names start with those letters remove their chairs and sing another song. Keep removing chairs until you feel you have balanced safety with the fun of lots of people sitting in each other's lap.

The Gift of the Game

No one wants to be kicked out of anything. For children, being kicked out of a game is equivalent to an adult being fired from a job. Doesn't feel good, does it? So why do we do it? Why do we need to play games that celebrate the one child who is always the fastest or the strongest? We don't. The smiles on children's faces when you tell them nobody will be kicked out of the game are joys to behold. With the rule that no one will be left out and there will be a place for everyone sit, children play this game less aggressively than traditional musical chairs. Some kindergarten teachers use this game to reinforce numbers by having the children count the various numbers of people sitting in the chairs. Children also learn how to touch and support others in a gentle and safe fashion. Once you engage in one round of cooperative musical chairs, you will never want to go back to the traditional way of playing it.

Soft Aggression

The third game component in the Creative Spirit continuum is soft aggression. This style of play must be carefully supervised for successful applications at school. Clearly, aggressive games are not appropriate or useful for certain grade levels or classes. People must master both creative and compassionate concepts before engaging in any aggressive activities. When the appropriate conditions are present, we believe that softly aggressive play can offer educational social skills to the students in your class.

Problems with Aggressive Play

Let's begin by looking at what does not work. The fact that kids have always played aggressive games is not a good reason to use such games at school. Just because your grandfather played dodgeball and your father played dodgeball doesn't mean you have to teach dodgeball to the next generation. It's an aggressive game. You throw things at people.

Dodgeball and many aggressive games are always popular with children who genetically mature faster than their peers. For them, these are the greatest games on the planet. These kids have the strength, coordination, and reflexes to protect their safety. Unfortunately, they prey upon others who are not their competitive equals. Those children, who are not as swift or fast, often have painful and intimidating game experiences. Students don't want to be hit so hard with the ball that it leaves a red mark or an impression of the ball manufacturer's name across their forehead. School curriculum cannot be designed just for the strongest and the swiftest.

If we were to draw a similar parallel to academics, third-grade math would be dominated by the brightest child who could do algebra. All math tests would cover problems trying to find out what x equals. Everyone but Amber, the math whiz, would fail. That's not the mission of elementary- and middle-school education. In most academics, we wisely try to include all students and not just focus on the smartest children. We must be just as wise when it comes to sports and other game activities.

Another example of missing the point concerning aggression happened at a school district that was having problems after high-school football games. After the game, players were expected to show their sportsmanship by forming handshake lines to congratulate the other team. Unfortunately, the players began to use the handshake lines to vent their aggression toward the other team by punching them as they passed by. This quickly escalated as players brought brass knuckles and small pieces of pipe to punch the other players with. These conflicts spilled over into parking lots and other parts of the community as the players sought vengeance by fighting.

This example is horrible as it stands. But to make matters worse, the people, including the administrative staff, who should have been acting as elders, chose to solve this problem by eliminating what they believed to be the source of the conflict, the evil and problematic handshake line.

They missed the point. In every game, players should be able to be good sports. If high school students can't play without fighting at the end of their game, the solution should have been to eliminate football and not the handshake line. After suspending one or more games, the coaches, players, and parents would have quickly figured out what was truly important about their football games: the people playing. This appropriate intervention would have focused on the actual problem, and the educational process of finding a solution would have developed important, life-serving skills.

Media coverage of professional sports often presents us with even worse examples of aggression. A future Hall of Fame pitcher threw a six-hitter one day, which for baseball is typically only a fair to good game. Yet he received four days of media coverage after he hit a batter with a 90-mile-per-hour fastball and the batter came up to the mound to fight him. The pitcher swiftly placed the batter in a head hold and then performed his celebrated "six-hitter" as he proceeded to hit him with his fist six times. That's not baseball—it's assault. Or what about an ice skater who hires someone to cripple her opponent by hitting her knee with a steel bar? That's not competitive edge—that's battery. A pro hockey player received eight penalties totaling fifty-one minutes for fighting, slashing, and other violent acts. The game is only sixty minutes long. This person wasn't playing hockey. He's wasn't even on the ice for 85 percent of the game. This player wasn't playing—he was just brawling. The most heinous event happened after a World Cup soccer player accidentally scored a goal for the other team. When he returned to his home country, he was shot. That's not frustrated fan response. That's murder.

All sports and games have not evolved from boxing. We've read the rules, and fighting just isn't there. Even in boxing they won't let you put an opponent in a head hold to hit him. Aggression that is out of control is not part of healthy play.

Healthy Solutions for Aggressive Play

To channel aggressive energies in a positive way, we must learn to control and soften their overall impact. When children regularly have practiced and internalized compassion and caring for every child in their class, then we begin to soften aggression. When they have practiced using nonabusive words to resolve hundreds of minor squabbles, we soften aggression. When students have taken the next growth step and learned how to prevent injuries and arguments, then the potential problems with aggression have been reduced significantly. These behaviors must be in place before we teach more specifically aggressive games, such as dodgeball.

Additionally, we soften aggression in all our play activities by building people-oriented rules into the games. Hard tags, feet tags, or accidentally hitting someone in the head with a ball just don't count as a tag or an out. Before playing aggressive games, children have practiced slow-motion tag, safety haven, detective, and rattlesnake tag. They've learned how to touch each other in compassionate and cooperative ways. We promote fairness with our kids by saying they can't tag, eliminate, or score on the players who are engaged in caring for someone. Teachers using our play concepts empower all the students to be accountable for their behaviors. The positive compliment sessions at the end of the games alter the actions for which children are praised in their play activities. These learned and reinforced social skills soften aggression.

Game equipment is essential to consider in softening aggression. We have chosen to use Nerf sponge balls when we play kick ball, soccer, or dodgeball because they are so kid-friendly.

Guidelines for Leading Soft Aggression Games

Be Vigilant and Maintain 100 Percent Control

Pay careful attention, observing all the students' actions and behaviors before, during, and after the game. Set limits or stop the game immediately when anything seems amiss. All the students in your class now trust that the elder supervising their activity will keep the game safe and fun.

Do Not Condone Horseplay

Horseplay often starts out playful and may look insignificant, but such teasing is often filled with aggressive cruelty. Behaviors like punching someone's arm often trigger biological responses beyond the superficial retort, "Nah-nah, didn't hurt at all." The adrenaline released may make the retaliatory punch harder than it was meant to be. Each successive event releases more and more biochemicals whose effect increases until horseplay becomes an actual fight. If the kids are horseplaying, announce, "I don't think we're ready for dodgeball today. We'll try again tomorrow when everyone shows that they are ready." Not playing a game is an effective way to teach healthy social skills. Don't stop playing completely. Just pick a different game that day, so the students can achieve success. It's their responsibility and your responsibility to intervene when they don't. Processing these disappointments will create quality learning.

Always Keep Your Focus on the People and Not on Winning

There's no score without people so keep the focus on what's important. If some players are driven to score regardless of the consequences to their peers, use individual time-outs or stop the game completely. Competition is wonderful, but it is only one of the twenty things the students said were important about play. At school, keep competition in balance. It is meant to be a *spice,* which can make things better. No one ever eats a whole plate of oregano by itself.

Anticipate Problems

One way you can use a soft-aggression game is to anticipate problems or failure. You may know that your class isn't ready, but it may be useful to choose a particular game some kids want to play, just to let it fail. We learn from our failures. Thomas Edison failed at creating thousands of filaments before he found the right one to illuminate the light bulb. Play is a safe arena where we can fail or struggle with our problems without momentous repercussions. When arguing or other expected incidents occur in a game, stop the play. At this point you can give concrete feedback to students on what they need to practice for a certain amount of time before you'll let them try the game again.

Successful Games Deserve Lots of Praise

When your game is played and it turns out to be fun, be sure to celebrate and reinforce specific behaviors you saw in specific students. Praising what goes well is the strongest teaching tool you have.

Add Humor

To soften aggressive and other acting out, add humor to foster buy-in and cooperation for all activities. When you attend one of our trainings, it is sidesplittingly apparent that we use a lot of shtick. And that's more than okay. After a training, we encourage participants to borrow our shtick or feel free to make up their own. Not only do humor and storytelling facilitate buy-in and cooperation, they really *soften* and set the tone for the kind of energies that children put out. Humor and story telling put scoring and competition in their proper place.

Keep Competition in a Healthy Perspective

Competition really is okay. It just needs to be placed in a healthy perspective. The only person you truly compete against is yourself. Also, the benefits of competition must not be gleaned at the expense of another person. Remember, *all* the people are the most important part of the game.

To begin softening aggression in our play activities, we must address the definition of competition. Our current definition originated during the Roman era, and it reflected conflicts between gladiators. Clearly, the perspective of "Winning isn't every thing; it's the only thing!" had a great deal of significance when competition was truly a matter of who would be alive for the next game. But this original idea regarding competition is now obsolete, like so many other beliefs that have changed radically over the past 2,000 years. We no longer play any sports or games to the death. It is therefore essential that we update and make relevant the meaning and focus of competition. Competition should now reflect a set of values far greater than an archaic and violent combat between gladiators.

Our new definition needs a foundation in the elements of life that *all* human beings compete and struggle with: time, space, and gravity. These are the universal factors we all face as challenges when we play.

Regarding the concept of time, we wonder: How fast can I swim 100 meters or run a marathon? How many points can a team score in four quarters, nine innings, or three periods? How quick are my reflexes? How long is my stamina? Am I a better chess player when I play by e-mail because the games may take weeks or months to complete? This is what our games actually reflect when we conceptualize ourselves as competing with or against time.

Space is our challenge with the infinite. Play is one way humans attempt to achieve brief mastery over the environment in which we live. How big should we make a basketball court or soccer field? How long or far should a foot race, a horse race, or an auto race be? How many squares on a checkerboard? Should we substitute a six-sided star for Chinese checkers? Should parallel bars be at the same height or uneven? Will our play space be ice, grass, or water? Inside or outdoors? In order to compete with space, we establish specific limits and parameters so we can measure and give meaning to what we have accomplished.

It is natural for us to strive against the ever-present force of gravity. Through our play we attempt to gain control of its confining bounds. How far can a football be kicked, a golf ball be hit, or a discus be thrown? Can I jump high enough to make a basket or do a triple toe loop? How much energy has the moon given the wave that I surf or the collision of tectonic plates given the mountain slope under my skis? Gravity is a fair, impartial, and equal competitor for everyone.

When we compete against time, space, and gravity, there's no need for violence and hostile aggression. People are simply demonstrating what they can accomplish. It allows each individual to see that, in reality, their competition is always against themselves and the natural elements. The question becomes, "Have I done the best that I can do?" If you want, you can compare the results of your play successes with others. However, this comparison is ultimately not necessary or relevant. For as you mix the dynamics of time, space, and gravity it becomes difficult to determine who or what is the best. Is the fastest runner the one who finishes first in the 100-meter, 1,500-meter, or 10,000-meter race? Do a swimmer, a hockey player, a skier, and a surfer compete equally with each other because they all do a sport that requires water? Is the best jumper a four-foot-ten-inch 90-pound gymnast who can do somersaults, flips, and turns and land without moving, or the six-foot-eight-inch 220-pound basketball player who can thunderously dunk a ball by leaping from the free-throw line?

Regardless of these comparisons, the focus of a new definition of competition is about what each living individual person can achieve. It's not about aggression, violence, and death. With our new understanding we can go back to the original Latin definition of competition and reinterpret its meaning. We no longer need to *struggle against* another. Our new definition can embrace *struggling together* with somebody against common forces of nature. This better exemplifies modern games such as chess, tennis, or golf, where people should be encouraged to work together to improve their skills rather than polarize into winners and losers. When we accept this perspective of competition, we are learning to play.

Regarding sports played as teams, we, as responsible elders, have a wonderful opportunity to help children get beyond our

Western cultural concept that the other team, the other players, are our enemies. Traditionally, that's how we are taught to perceive and treat the people of the other team. If we think of them as our enemies, we can feel more comfortable hurting them. At school, at work, and in our neighborhoods, we must teach the idea that the other team is just our *opposition* and is made up of people like us. We should honor and respect our opposition and be glad that our opposition showed up, because without them we would have a boring game. Be concrete with your students. Ask them, "Who would chase after the kick ball if you didn't have the other team? Who would pitch to you?" Focus must be placed on fun and people and much less importance placed on competition and scoring. This revolutionary thought brings great benefits.

An insightful and creative woman named Ann Herbert has written a wonderful piece of satire. We were excited when we read it. She puts the concepts of scoring, competition, and playfulness into humorous perspective. We'd like to share it with you. It's called "The Art of Play":

> In the beginning, God didn't make just two people, he (she) made a bunch of us because he wanted us to have a lot of fun. And he said you really can't have fun unless there's a whole gang of you. So he put us in Eden, which was a combination garden and playground and park, and told us to have fun. At first, we did have fun, just like he expected. We rolled down the hills. We waded in the streams. We climbed on the trees, we swung on the vines, ran in the meadows. We frolicked in the woods. We hid in the forest and acted silly. We laughed a lot.
>
> Then, one day, this snake told us we weren't having real fun because we weren't keeping score. Back then, we didn't know what "score" was. When he explained it, we still couldn't see the fun. But he said we should give an apple to the person who was best of all the games and that we would never know who was best without keeping score. Well, we could all see the fun of that because we were *all* sure that we were *all* the best.
>
> Oh, it was different after that. We yelled a lot. We had to make up

new scoring rules for most of the games. Others, like frolicking, we stopped playing because they were just too hard to score.

By the time God found out what had happened, we were spending about forty-five minutes a day actually playing, and the rest of the time, we were working out scoring. God was wroth about that—very, very wroth. He said we couldn't use his garden anymore because we weren't having fun. We told him we were having lots of fun. He was just being narrow-minded because it wasn't exactly the kind of fun he originally thought of. But God wouldn't listen. He kicked us out and he said we couldn't come back to the garden until we stopped keeping score. To rub it in, to get our attention, he told us we were all going to die and that our scores wouldn't mean anything, anyhow.

But he was wrong. My cumulative all-game score is 16,548, and that means a lot to me. And if I can raise it to 20,000 before I die, I'll know that I've accomplished something. And even if I can't, my life still has a great deal of meaning because I've taught my children to score high, and they'll be able to reach 20,000 or even 30,000.

Really, it was life in the garden that didn't mean anything. Fun is great in its place, but without scoring there's no reason for it. God actually has a very superficial view of life, and I'm certainly glad my children are being raised away from his influence. We were all lucky. We were all very grateful to the snake.

We believe the snake has given us a really bum deal. I personally don't know what my score was at the end of the kick-ball game in my third-grade class on October 19, 1960. I do know whether I was able to make friends. I do remember if I was liked or not. No one remembers scores years after the event. In fact, ask anyone what the score was in the Superbowl game five years ago. Most people can't even remember who played, much less what the score was. At the time it seemed so very important, but what remains are the feelings, not the numbers. And so it is with children when they play. It is more meaningful to remember feeling good, accepted, and respected than 7 to 15.

Good sportsmanship is presented by our media, but positive examples are reported far less often than examples of poor sportsmanship, aggression, and violence. We need more examples like the following, which were reported by National Public Radio:

The National Cuban Baseball League, winners of the Olympic gold medal in Barcelona, demonstrated that though they play to win, all players are important and celebrated even when they are on the other team. When the Cuban pitcher accidentally hit the batter with a curve ball, he and the managers of both teams immediately went to the batter to see if he was okay. They enacted rule number one! Also, when a member of the opposing team made a good play, they publicly applauded their opponents' skills.

Another touching story was when two Japanese Olympic athletes scored the same points in an Olympic event. At that time, the Olympic Committee did not have a process for two athletes coming up with the same score, so they randomly gave one the silver medal and the other the bronze. However, on their return to Japan, each athlete had his medal cut down the middle and presented the other with a half. They then had the halves fused together, so each one could have an equal silver-and-bronze "medal of eternal friendship."

This is what being a good sport is all about. Only when the focus of game stays firmly on the people can aggressive games be fun, exciting, and useful.

Soft Aggression Activities

BE MY FRIEND, ONE, TWO, THREE

(Third grade and up, ten or more players, a large safe playing space, no equipment)

How It's Played

This is a soft-aggression game that can be played with lots of enthusiasm and energy. Mark off a large space (approximately 100 by 40 feet if you have twenty-five players). Have everyone stand on one of the long sides of the field, and pick two boys and two girls to be the first set of friends. These four players go to the inside of the playing area and begin the chant, "Lonely people standing there, won't you be my friend?" At the end of the chant, the people on the side race across the playing field, trying to reach the other side without being caught. The friends in the middle attempt to "catch" the running players and must touch them long enough to say the phrase, "Be my friend, one, two, three." If contact is maintained, the person touched becomes one of the friends and helps catch other people. Eventually, everyone becomes part of the group of friends. At the end of the round, the two original boys pick two new girls and the original girls pick two new boys, and the game starts over.

The Gift of the Game

The gift of this game came from its metamorphosis over the years that we have played it in its various incarnations. Initially, we observed a game called British bulldog. British bulldog happens to be a brutal activity with questionable usefulness. Mostly, children just got hurt trying to break through the arms of the players in the middle. We eliminated the action of breaking through people's arms. Instead, we had players try to pick other players up off the ground. The game was renamed American eagle to disassociate the play from British bulldog. The game still proved unsatisfactory for many players, so we then changed from picking people up to having prolonged tags. This improved the game significantly, yet there was still an aspect of uncontrolled aggression as people raced by, thinking they were unstoppable American eagles. The last piece we needed to shape this soft-aggressive game into one that reminded us that all the players were really our friends was a change in title. Be my friend, one, two, three conveys the right message while providing plenty of physical action.

BALLOON SOCCER

(Third grade and up, twelve or more people, an inside open space, a bunch of balloons at least twelve inches in diameter)

How It's Played

This is a moderate soft-aggressive activity. First, blow up your balloons and store them (in a balloon corral) away from the game. Define a clear space of approximately 20 by 20 feet. Set two sturdy chairs (the goals) at opposite sides and encircle the chairs with cones or some other boundary marker, like tape on the floor. Randomly divide into two teams and have players *sit* on the floor. Be sure to scatter the members of each team all over the playing area, and have one player from each team sit in each goalie chair.

The object of the game is to tap the balloons to your own goalie, who must pop the balloon using his fingers. Instruct goalies to pop balloons far away from their own and others' faces. Do *not* allow sharp objects, such as pens or needles, to be used to pop the balloons, for obvious safety reasons. All players must keep their *bottoms* on the floor at all times, and they cannot rise on their knees to get an extra height advantage. Players may scoot around to get to different positions, but they cannot crawl, stand, or roll around to get there. The balloons can only be tapped by the hand. For safety reasons, kicking, carrying, or holding a balloon is not permitted. The goalie must stay seated in the chair while trying to catch a balloon that is being tapped toward them. The boundary area around the goalie is a safe zone. Players may reach into the safe zone with their arms to deflect the balloons from the goalie. However, they may not scoot their bodies into the safe zone. Adjust the size of the safe zone to meet your students' needs.

Many variations are possible in this game. First of all, players don't have to pop the balloons to make a score. This makes the game last longer and cost less. Also, kids who are uncomfortable around loud noises may not like popping balloons. Some balloons will pop during play, so be prepared and have some extras. Try having two or more balloons in play at a time. This becomes especially funny when the goalie is holding several balloons yet still tries to catch another. Many a goalie has lost several caught balloons while trying to get another. Have the goalies wear blindfolds or close their eyes to make scoring even harder. Having fixed positions where the players are not allowed to move may be a necessary step to take if you want to slow the action down or if some players become too rowdy. Always explain why you are making such changes, so that the children can learn from the experience.

We've tried this game standing up, and it's just not as safe. Players got too excited jumping around and accidentally hurt each other. We found the only safe, soft-aggressive way to play this game was to start and stay on the floor. Once again, sharp objects to pop the balloons are not allowed.

The Gift of the Game

We like this soft-aggressive activity because it's perfect to blow off energy on a day when you can't get outside. It helps kids practice setting boundaries around their bodies. They also learn how to stay in control while still playing hard with other people and with objects in a room. Be sure to allow time for the teams to plan some offensive and defensive strategies. We are amazed at the inventive ideas that groups create, especially if they have played this game five or six times.

There is so much action going on in balloon soccer that it is almost impossible to know what the score is after the first few pops. We love using this method to deemphasize scoring: At the beginning of the game, we tell each team that they will receive a point for every balloon that their goalie pops. When all but one remaining balloon has been popped, we explain to the whole group that the other balloons were really just practice and that the final balloon we are holding is the only one that really counts. We then set up an impossible task, saying, "Both teams only have five seconds to pop this last balloon or the game ends in a tie." Nine out of ten times the balloon remains unpopped, and the children are satisfied with the tie score. This game generates so much laughter.

TRIAD

(Third grade and up, four or more players, an open play area, no equipment)

How It's Played

We don't know of a game that has as much flexible teamwork or can tire you out as fast as triad. Have players form groups of four. (If there are extra players allow some of the groups to have five.) Three of the players in each group join hands and form a triad (in the larger groups of five, four people join hands to make a quad). The remaining player becomes the challenger.

The object of this game is for the challenger to tag one of the players of the triad. Easier said than done. The game starts by having the challenger announce to the triad who she will try to tag. The triad will adjust to move that person farthest away from the challenger. Now play begins. The challenger moves left, moves right, tries to crawl underneath, gets back up, and goes around and around, but each time the triad moves to protect the player the challenger is after. Any tag counts. When the challenger finally catches the person, they trade places, and the new challenger announces who he is after. Play continues until everyone has a turn being chased and being the challenger. One special rule is that the members of the triad should not let go of one another's hands. If this happens, it counts as a tag for the challenger. Obviously, the challenger cannot pull the hands of the triad players apart.

Modifying the triads makes for extra fun and protects everyone's self-esteem. If the challenger has been unable to tag the person she is after, try having members of the triad hop on one leg. Another idea is to have the players who are doing the protecting close their eyes and be directed by the person the challenger is after. Let your group have multiple triads and multiple challengers. Use marker handkerchiefs to identify the target players in each triad, and let any challenger catch any target person. Always keep the games safe, and use this activity to support teamwork between all the different players.

The Gift of the Game

After years of playing triad, I thought that this game was primarily useful to ventilate pent-up physical energies. I had discovered

Triad

that kids spent so much energy playing the game, even for only two to eight minutes, that triad was the perfect activity for older students who were acting restless. But as I've been reminded and over again, don't underestimate the people's inventiveness in deriving gains from a game.

We were playing with a group of third graders on the fourth day of the school year. There was a new student from China who had only been in the United States for three weeks and didn't speak English. She colored as the class discussed the values of play, and she barely followed along as we went to the playground to play some games.

First we tried "Like, totally it" tag. She stood there, never moved an inch, and looked kind of scared. Wanting to get her involved, I then tried safety haven. Surely, I thought, the concept of hugging and humming would get her involved. She didn't understand a word I said. Failing to convince her by a simple hum-hug demonstration, I had the whole class hum and hug while facing her. Again, she showed no understanding and continued to look afraid, but we went ahead and played the game. In this instance, safety haven, which had always worked at bringing children together, did not succeed. Maybe next time.

A little flustered, I suggested we play triad. What was I thinking? This activity is too physical. It might only scare her more. Oh, well, I'll just have her watch, I thought to myself. Everyone broke up into groups of four, except three girls who seemed to be close friends and this little girl from China. I decided to gently move them together to make a triad of girls holding hands with the remaining girl the challenger. I announced to the class to begin, and to my surprise there was all this giggling and laughing streaming out of our Asian friend's mouth. In fact, her whole group was running this way and that way, laughing and giggling. Just like that, she had shown the others a language they all knew. With each passing moment, the bond between the group grew stronger.

After the game, the class expressed their positive feelings with each other. Once again, she didn't know what we were saying, and no one gave her any compliments. But the game had worked its magic. As we started to walk back to the class, the other three students put her between them and held hands again. They immediately resumed laughing and giggling. I felt overjoyed watching them swing their arms back and forth as they crossed the playground. They were no longer strangers.

For the rest of the day the four of them spent time teaching languages to each other. The girls would race up to the teacher and relate each breakthrough. "She said *pizza*." "She said my name!" Later in the day, her older brother, who spoke English, translated for her. He said this was the first day she had enjoyed being at school. She liked having friends. The whole class won that day because of how those four students played together.

OH, FIDO

(Any grade, ten to forty students, inside, sturdy chairs)

How It's Played

Arrange all the players in a circle, sitting in chairs. Ask someone in your class to give you the name of their pet. Let's say the child has a dog they call Fido. Then that becomes the title of your game: oh, Fido. Select one player to be it. Remove her chair from the game and have her stand in the middle of the circle. The object of this game is for the person in the middle to get a chair.

Movement in oh, Fido occurs when two players who are sitting down make eye contact with each other and make a nonverbal agreement to exchange chairs. When they think the person in the middle isn't looking, they get up and try to switch places. If the person in the middle sees them move, he can try to beat the players to one of the empty chairs. Often there are several people making chair switches at the same time, which causes confusion and usually allows the person in the middle to find a seat. More action happens because other players can get up and sit in an empty seat while the players are trying to make a switch.

To protect the self-esteem of the player in the middle in case she can't get a chair, we give her special power. At any time, she can yell the name of the game, "Oh, Fido!" and everyone sitting down has to get up and move at least two chairs away from where he or she started.

Practice safety! We always make a rule that if someone touches a chair first, it becomes that person's chair. This reduces the number of people colliding and crashing into chairs. If students are knocking each other down while running around, you may want to slow the game down by making everyone walk heel-to-toe. Or you can stop the game and have the kids offer suggestions.

The Gift of the Game

The naming aspect of this activity can give gifts to a child even before the game has started. Being chosen to name this activity em-

Oh, Fido

powers and acknowledges the child. This can help to gently quiet attention-seeking children who become relaxed and less anxious when they are recognized. Or maybe you want to boost the self-esteem of the isolated or ostracized child. Giving her a chance to name the game validates her. This often tears down another group barrier and "de-cootiefies" this child as the group learns more about her. You also might reserve the naming of this activity for the child who has been the most nurturing to her peers. This action always reinforces the positive peer culture.

The rule that the person in the middle can yell out, "Oh, Fido," when unable to get a seat goes a long way. Some children don't possess the skills, cunning, or power to get themselves out of impossible situations. Using creative-play dynamics to make up rules like this one enables *all* children to play this aggressive game. Kids who are fast won't need to yell, "Oh, Fido," because they will probably always get a seat quickly. For children who are a bit slower, this is a safety valve to protect their self-image when they think they need to use it. When children can trust that their humanity and skills will be honored and taken into account, they will feel better able to take risks. We also like how this game gently assists in developing eye contact and other nonverbal communication skills.

OFF BALANCE

(Fifth grade and older, groups of two players, space to stand, no equipment)

How It's Played

This is an aggressive activity, but it can help players learn to control their physical energy. Begin by having everyone find a partner. Partners stand about two feet apart with their feet directly under their shoulders. Players raise their hands in front of their bodies with their arms slightly flexed. The object of off balance is for students to rapidly push at their opponents' hands, making them lose balance and move their feet. It might seem like strength will always prevail in such a contest, but it's not so. A highly effective strategy is to avoid hand contact with the opponent, so he topples forward and moves his feet. Only the hands can be used as a target area. A player may not push an opponent in the chest, shoulders, or head.

The Gift of the Game

I find this game useful because it so carefully controls the act of aggression. Players clearly have to face and look at their opponent. It becomes obvious that they need their opponents, or they would look silly standing there alone thrusting their hands into the air. Opponents are good! Without them there are few games. To control aggression only one target area can be attacked. When they play, kids hear the slapping together of the hands. This has the sound of aggression, yet the actual physical impact causes less discomfort than enthusiastic clapping. I especially like the lesson of the game, which teaches that excessive aggression is not successful. Students learn that when they passively stand there with their knees bent slightly and give their arms no tension at all. Using this dynamic, opponents will never push them off balance.

Off balance

DRAGONS DODGEBALL

(Fourth grade and older, ten to forty players, large playing area free of breakables, Nerf balls)

How It's Played

Start by having the players form a large circle. For every ten players in the game, select two to become dragons. Each member of your two-player dragon group(s) must decide who will be the head and who will be the tail of the dragon. The tail person holds the shoulders or the waist of the front person. The dragons roam around in the center of the circle.

The object of the game is for the players of the circle to throw the Nerf balls and hit the tail person of the dragon in the *butt*. *Only* the *butt* counts. The player who hits a dragon's butt moves into the circle to become the new tail of the dragon. The previous tail now becomes the head of the dragon. The former head of the dragon returns to the circle, and the game continues. It is not easy to hit the tail of a dragon, because the head person is always trying to move so that no one can get a clean throw at the tail person. Teamwork is essential, and we usually have a three-second rule to encourage players of the circle to pass to someone else quickly if they don't have a clear shot. It is useful to have two to four balls in action.

Remember, throwing things at people is aggressive. Quickly stop play if players are throwing violently or too hard. All the players have to do is hit the dragon's butt. They are not trying to knock anyone out. We also make a rule that too hard a throw just doesn't count. This will help players learn that the people, not the scoring, are what is really important.

The Gift of the Game

Overall, we're not too keen on dodgeball. It's an aggressive game easily misused. You're throwing something hard at others. If you've got cannon arms and lightning reflexes, then this game is fun for you. If you are like the rest of us, most likely you're not enjoying being pummeled by a hard rubberized basketball traveling at the speed of sound. Sometimes we think that we teach kids dodgeball because our parents taught us dodgeball, their parents taught them dodgeball, and so on. Well, we finally can teach our children a dodgeball game where they can learn and practice compassion, empathy, and teamwork. You can pick your jaws off the floor now. We were surprised and grateful to discover Terry Orlick's dragons dodgeball. A child learns not to throw the balls hard as they very quickly discover that if they are successful with their throwing tag, their butt will become the next target. That golden rule, do on to others as you would have them do on to you, is concretely evident in this game. Compassion and empathy emerge victorious. Teamwork comes into action because the head of the dragon will protect its rear by foiling clear shots. That factor, plus the three-second holding rule, encourages players to share the ball with someone on the other side of the circle who has a clearer shot. Finally, we always suggest using soft Nerf balls. If throwing still becomes rough, help children solve this issue by ultimately having the students who are making hard throws play with their non-dominant hand or throw underhand rather than take time-outs.

STRATEGY TAG

(Fourth grade and older, ten or more players, outside or in a gym, no equipment)

How It's Played

Ever feel like everyone is trying to get you? Well, this game playfully lives up to that feeling. Players begin by standing shoulder to shoulder in a straight line. Now have every other person turn and face the opposite direction so that the line has a person facing forward, backward, forward, backward, and so on. The people in line are called chasers. A quarry and one chaser are chosen from the group to start the game.

The object of the game is for the two, active players to run around the line as the chaser attempts to catch the quarry. The problem for the quarry is that the chaser can choose a replacement from the line at any time to continue the chase for her. In order to pick a replacement, the chaser comes up from *behind* and *taps* another player on his back. The player who was tapped steps forward and becomes the new chaser while the previous chaser steps into the vacant spot the other player just left. Eventually, the chaser catches the quarry. Once tagged, the roles immediately reverse. The chaser becomes a new quarry. The quarry becomes the chaser and can use the line of players as replacements.

Only the chaser can tap someone as a replacement. The quarry is stuck running away from the chaser until he is caught and the roles reverse. Players must stay within twelve feet of the line at all times. Players running around the line can change directions at any time. Have fun and remember this game takes strategy.

The Gift of the Game

Teamwork: It's on every poster that we make in the classrooms. This is a perfect game to allow children to practice the teamwork they think they believe in. Initially, your class will have long, drawn-out races between two students who refuse to give up chasing each other. You will probably have to invent rules like, "You

Strategy tag

can't circle the line more than three times without picking a replacement." Players actually make the game more difficult when they don't use the line. Eventually, children will learn that the excitement and pace of the game improves when they use each other. At this point, the insight about the simplest form of teamwork will have been accomplished. With a lot of practice, your class will transfer this learning to other sports, such as kick ball, soccer, and basketball. This awareness should help stop that one player who will race all over the field trying to make every play alone. Remember to return to and use your posters to help the children focus and perform the values they identified about play.

ACCUMULATOR

(Fourth grade and older, eight or more players, large outside or inside area free of breakables, three Nerf balls)

How It's Played

The object of accumulator is to accumulate all the lost friends, thus making them all winners. Begin by setting up your boundaries, which should be the size of a basketball court. Select two to four

Accumulator

players to start as the accumulators. The accumulators take possession of the Nerf balls in the center of the playing area. The lost friends scatter to the outskirts, as far away as they can get from the people with the balls. The game starts when the accumulators. say, "*Hasta la vista,* baby!" Accumulators may throw the balls to hit any lost friend, turning her into another accumulator. The newly captured accumulators now assist in gathering everyone else.

Accumulators do have one major challenge. When they are *holding* a ball, they cannot run or move their feet. However, accumulators without the ball can move freely on the playing field. The best strategy is for the accumulators without a ball to get close to or surround a lost friend and then have the ball-holding, feet-frozen accumulator(s) pass a ball to them for a successful short throw. Long throws usually miss, and the accumulators can spend a lot of time chasing after the erratic balls. Teamwork is the essence of this game.

Instruct the accumulators that they should keep one arm waving in the air so all accumulators are easily identified for ball passing and teamwork. Fair-play rule: Only the accumulators may raise their hands and shout that they are accumulators.

There is a lot of action in this one, but lost friends can only be turned into accumulators if they are hit between the knees and the shoulders. Head and feet hits don't count for obvious safety reasons. If someone is hit too hard, the tag won't count, and the thrower will need to stay with the injured person until he or she feels ready to play again.

The Gift of the Game

No one likes getting kicked out of a game, and here people are accumulated, not eliminated. Sometimes children learn the value of teamwork when it's missing. We recall many classes who became frustrated that the same three dominant or skilled kids were hogging the ball. Often these greedy ballplayers were the ones who sent the balls flying outside boundary lines without accumulating more lost friends. The frustrated children who were tired of chasing wayward balls could ask that the game stop. During the processing time, they identified solutions so that everyone could be included and every lost friend would be turned into an accumulator.

Remember that your group has not failed if it needs to stop a game that is not working out well. Often this is the point where most of the learning occurs, where most behavior changes begin. Try to see discomfort and frustration as tools. Never lose sight of the fact that most positive behavioral changes occur after children become comfortable with their uncomfortable feelings. Using these simple games, you can help schoolchildren overcome their difficulties with teamwork. You can appreciate why Jean Piaget and Erik Erickson advocate team sports for seventh graders and older children.

BLOB

(Third grade and older, eight to forty players, very large playing area, no equipment)

How It's Played

This is an accumulation tag game of blobs and amoebas. Blobs know life is better when there are lots of friends hanging together.

Blob

Amoebas think life is fine alone and celebrate the freedom of individuality. The object of the game is for the blobs to catch all the free amoebas. Select a large rectangular playing area about 60 by 100 feet, and start the game by picking one person to become a blob for every seven people playing the game. The blobs start a three-two-one countdown, and each blob, acting independently from the other blobs, begins chasing the amoebas all over the playing field. If a blob touches an amoeba, that amoeba becomes part of that blob by holding hands with the person who tagged her. The blobs grow and grow every time another amoeba is caught.

Teamwork and cooperation are essential. If the blob comes apart while they are chasing someone, the tag does not count. Moving slowly, stretching out, and chasing one specific amoeba at a time are all good strategies. Amoebas may not break through or run between the members of the blob. At some point near the end of the game, several blobs may wish to connect, making one huge blob that stretches across the entire playing field. This makes rounding up the last few amoebas simple work if the blob walks down the field, not letting anyone get past its ends.

The Gift of the Game

To discover what it is like to be really, really excited without losing self-control and awareness is a fantastic gift for children and teenagers. To discover that effective strategies and teamwork can get the job accomplished more efficiently is another valuable lesson to be gleaned from this game. As the game facilitator, be aware that this game is difficult for most young children the first time they try it. Don't give up. Help your children explore solutions of cooperation and teamwork. The successes they gain with repeated play cultivate their abilities to work collectively with others. Can you see how we have further redefined the role of the players in all our games by regularly calling them "friends"? This is a social-skills education that is lived and not just read in a conflict-resolution program.

Also, if you want to teach some practical applications of geometry, play blob. My favorite tactic is to have my blob chain choose the fastest kid in the class to catch. I tell my blob, "We will walk while our amoeba quarry will have to jog or run." My blob members all like this idea. "In fact," I tell my blob, "we will chase this amoeba until it is so tired that it will ask to be tagged, on purpose, just so it can walk with us." And that's what usually happens.

Here's how this strategy works. Our blob will move to the center of the field and begin chanting the name of our amoeba quarry. The person closest to the center remains almost stationary while the other blob members move like a door on a hinge, forcing our quarry to stay outside our reach. To avoid us, the amoeba must jog or run in a circle about ten feet away from us. This extra ten feet really changes the distance the amoeba must travel to stay out of reach. When the amoeba reverses direction, the blob simply yells, "Switch," as we all let go of one another's hands, turn around, reconnect hands, and then walk in the opposite direction. For advanced-math connections to your class's game of blob, try having your class measure different circle circumferences with a string or calculate the distances.

SPONGE WARS

(Third grade and up, best played with a lot of players, outdoors, two sponges or more per player and two water buckets)

How It's Played

Set up a playing space about the size of a basketball court outdoors, and place a boundary line across the middle. Place the safety bases (buckets of wet sponges) in the middle of the opposite end lines of the playing area. Divide players, using a double divide, into two teams and place the teams in their half of the playing area. Be firm on the rule that players from opposite teams *cannot* cross the middle line or they'll become frozen solid at the point where they crossed.

Players will try to tag opposing team members with laser blasts. Laser blasts are represented by thrown wet sponges. If a player is hit by a laser blast, he becomes stunned or frozen. Once hit, frozen players cannot move (that is, pick up or throw sponges) and are at the mercy of players on the other team, who can continue to *softly* bombard them with wet sponges. Frozen players are permitted to turn and face away from the opposing team, so they will only be hit with sponges from behind. Fortunately, each team will choose a "healer," who becomes the *only* person on their team with the amazing ability to unfreeze frozen teammates. When a healer touches a frozen player, the player is free to move again. Players can be frozen and unfrozen any number of times. Prior to the start of the game, teams must announce (using lots of fanfare) to the opposition just who their healer is.

Because of his or her great thawing abilities, the healer is the most important player on a team. If the healers are hit by a sponge, they are removed from the game because no one has the power to unfreeze the healers. If a team's healer is tagged with a sponge, it loses a great strategic advantage. From that point, none of their frozen players can be thawed out. So it is a very important team strategy to choose one or two players to act as shields to protect

Sponge wars

their healer. Explain that a player who becomes frozen should turn around and call out for his healer. The healer, protected by her human shield, goes to the frozen player, tags him, and lets him reenter the game as an active players. As long as the healer is touching her shield(s), the shield(s) can't be frozen because his healer's touch is constantly unfreezing him. If a healer accidentally becomes separated from her bodyguard, the healer should immediately run back to her safety base (the bucket of wet sponges). Healers are only safe from the laser blasts of wet sponges if they are touching their water-bucket safety base.

If a healer is tagged with a wet sponge while not on the safety bucket, we recommend taking a brief time-out. All action must cease. Remove the healer and all currently frozen players on the frozen healer's team from the court. They will now root and cheer their remaining teammates from the sidelines. From this point on, any player on that team when hit by a sponge must leave the playing area. Remember, they have no healer left to unfreeze them. When there are only five players left on a team, the other team has only thirty seconds to "sponge" the remaining players or the game ends as a tie.

Most games end in a draw, but don't worry if a single team wins. By the time you are ready to play sponge wars with your group of children they should have had a great deal of practice in healthy social skills. So they should be able to tolerate this dynamic without teasing and taunting. Plus, there will be an advantage given to the "losing" team when you start the game over. At the end of a game, the losing team usually has a lot of extra sponges on their side of the playing field. They get to keep them. Yahoo! The other team cannot cross the middle line to get these sponges. You can reassure the team with few sponges that they'll have plenty of sponges in their territory real soon after the game begins again.

Reminder: Be sure that all the players understand completely that people are the most important part of the game and that vicious, aggressive acts and rule breaking will not be tolerated *before, during,* or *after* the game. Be sure all rules, concepts, and boundaries are established and explained before letting teams pick up their wet laser blasts. Before and after each game, no throwing of sponges is allowed. Be especially firm with the rule that even players on the same team cannot attack each other with water or sponges. Always start the game with everyone counting down, "Five, four, three, two, one, go." Now go have fun!

The Gift of the Game

We have often described this game as the carrot in front of the pony. When we do trainings at schools, there are always children around who watch their teachers play our games. No other game we play excites the students as much as watching their principal, teachers, and parents throw wet sponges at each other. The students' response is always, "When do *we* get to play sponge wars?" The excitement about playing this game often becomes a catalyst for teaching the social skills, values, and responsibilities that must be mastered before engaging in a soft-aggression activity. Sponge wars is intentionally placed at the end of our trainings and at the end of this book. It will not succeed without a strong framework and understanding of creativity, compassion, and soft aggression by all the participants. When your children have earned the opportunity to play this game, they will truly possess the skills to have fun with all the people in a safe and enthusiastic manner.

Learning-to-Play Tips for the Classroom

1. Start the *Learning to Play* process by creating the two posters: "Why do we play?" and "What is the most important part of every game?" During the discussion that follows the first question, encourage students to express how they like to feel during play. Continue to strongly reinforce the number-one answers of "fun" and "people." Use the posters regularly to point out the positive experiences in the children's games.
2. Discuss the two rules. Rule 1 is that if someone is hurt, the person closest to him *must stop* and check to see if he is okay and stay with him until he feels better. Rule 2 is that people with disagreements or arguments must leave the game and settle their issues before coming back to play. Make posters for both hall and doorways, so kids see these messages just before they go out to play. (It's always appropriate to remind the students that the school conduct codes apply and that fighting, pushing, swearing, and yelling are not permitted.)

3. Teach and foster student responsibility. Set up a student game-planning committee for each week. Allow students (with your supervision) to determine the activities. When picking the weekly group, try to have a mix of students that like a variety of activities.
4. Turn over the nomination/compliment sessions to the student leader of the day. This processing of good feelings must be part of the allotted time to play. Feedback from almost every school indicates that this is one of the most important parts of every school day.
5. Start your classes off with active games that focus on *equality* and *trust*. We recommend "Like, totally it" tag as a warm-up game almost every day. Others, like safety haven, triple tag, rattlesnake tag, magic shoe, and peace patrol and gremlins set a good tone for everyone to feel included. These are also terrific games for students to observe how well they are doing with playing by the rules, being honest, and caring for each other. Just as you do in other academic areas, anticipate some regression over the summer, and don't start in the fall with the most aggressive or competitive games. Use some name-recognition games such as Rumplestiltskin or cosmic motions at the beginning of school.
6. Play to have fun! Stop all unsafe, nonproductive games. Sticking with a torturous activity for the full period is not useful. Teachers across the country say this is one of our most helpful concepts. When necessary, calmly process with the class what is not working well and allow the students to suggest ways to improve the situation. Many classes have determined that certain games cannot be played for a while. Banning an activity for a short period seems to be an effective incentive for students to practice the desired social behaviors successfully in other games. They can later return to the game that was a problem. Sometimes it works, and sometimes the children see that they still haven't mastered certain social skills, and the game is put on hold again.

7. We highly recommend using older students in the school to model and lead activities with younger grades. It takes some coordination to identify student groups who will adopt a class and attend their play periods on a regular basis. It promotes the positive peer-pressure model that principals and teachers advocate by demonstrating the social skills expected at a higher grade level.
8. In class, have a monthly curriculum assignment where students write and describe different positive values that they demonstrated or observed during play. Stress that they write about honesty, friendship, caring, cooperation, trust, competition, sportsmanship, and other values. Send these assignments to the editor of the local or school newspaper.

   In younger grades, use these same topics for verbal expression during show-and-tell, such as, "Tell about a nice time you had playing at home with ______." Or divide the class into partners and have each partner write the other a note about a time that he saw her play nicely. Read the notes and do a process session with the class.
9. Have one or more art projects each year that focus on healthy play at school, at home, and elsewhere. Put them in the hallway for everyone to see.
10. Plan a parent-student game night, and let the parents have some fun with their kids. All ages can easily play together. Have a group of students (with parent or teacher support) become the leaders for this event.

Conclusion: The Role of Play in Education

So many schools have been held hostage by children's arguments turning into fights that their only recourse has been to ban or avoid play. This doesn't resolve the problem any more than the ostrich evades things by putting its head in the sand. It is essential that we teach children how to communicate and negotiate their differences, and the ideal way to practice these social skills is through play.

Contemporary entertainment, video games, and professional sport competitions are not exposing children to the values or techniques necessary for them to grow into successful problem solvers. Conflicts between kids and their electronic games require no communication at all. The game is always right, and the child expediently terminates the issue by hitting the restart button and beginning again. Often the children learn manipulative secrets to bypass such difficulties, and they see knowing this manipulation as a skill. Kids need to learn much more useful, realistic, and effective communication patterns to become successful adults. Conflicts between peers is person-to-person, not person-to-machine. Often who is right or not is not what matters in a disagreement between people. How we argue may be more important than who is right or wrong. Can we argue or disagree with one another fairly? Sometimes both of the people disagreeing are right.

The models of professional sports competitions complicate conflict-resolution skills because the outcome of these events is based on making money. Values like fairness, honesty, and compassion are quickly left behind when the potential for millions of dollars is at stake. The mock solution to professional sports disagreements has been the development of referees, the sports police. Admittedly, these "objective" observers are intended to monitor the rules and conduct of the players, and we believe they try their best. Unfortunately, this process is loaded with flaws. The worst consequence of the referee system is that personal responsibility is significantly diminished. Even when two players know what really happened, a referee can see it differently, and that's what counts. Players must attempt to rationalize these injustices, hoping that the imperfect referees will make another error, which might balance things out.

What's even worse for children to see is that rule infractions don't really count unless you are caught. Intimidation and fighting are condoned in this system until it goes too far out of control. The referee police system seems like a creation developed by children who never matured. Watching this system teaches children to emulate these tantrums, verbal abuses, and violent acts of aggression when they have conflicts during play. And that's often what we see at school. The vast majority of students in school settings will never be million-dollar athletes. So why do we teach or play by their rules?

There is a more useful approach!

Learning to Play, Playing to Learn and the Healthy Play Is a Solution program put game disagreements and other problematic situations in a helpful perspective. Our process is open to everyone—teachers, students, community leaders, recreation technicians (people who work for city or county park and recreation departments or in after-school programs), playground monitors, and parents. The games presented in this book become tools for practicing the people-friendly philosophies and rules. They become the arena in which both inconsequential and important matters teach our children valuable personal relationship skills. Who's it or not it will be quickly forgotten when students have learned how to make peaceful compromises. What will emerge from the games will be a greater sense of responsibility and community. We will pay more attention to ourselves and to each other. We will identify with each other's failures and triumphs. We will create greater tolerances for our differences and even celebrate them. We will also see more clearly how we are all alike. What will become paramount in our lives will be the process of growing as thoughtful and feeling people and sharing our loving relationships with those who encompass us. We will know joy, and we will stand a chance for peace.

We hope that the information and materials presented in this book will challenge you and encourage you to see that the world can be a better place if we take action. And who says our actions have to be dull or boring? We can live to have fun!

Never stop laughing.

Never stop playing.

Peacefully yours,
Charlie Steffens and Spencer Gorin

Special Addendum: Learning to Play at Home

Although the majority of our text has been devoted to using play in an educational setting, our overall belief about play is that it belongs everywhere. In reality, all people are both teachers and students when it comes to play. Focusing on an educational format has enabled us to explain lessons of critical importance within a larger social setting before bringing play back home where it belongs.

The Playful Family

Using play with your family is easy. You will find that the games described in this book are perfect for children's birthday parties, for teen sleep-overs, long car trips, vacations, family picnics, holiday gatherings, and daily use. Think of this section as a crash course on general rules for smaller groups. Use your new knowledge of creative-play concepts, presented earlier in this book, to modify any game to meet your family's requirements. For example, imagine you are having a small birthday party of ten children and want to play sponge wars. Unfortunately, it is raining outside and you don't want to have the neighborhood children tossing wet sponges at each other in the house, demolishing your favorite picture of Uncle Elmo while trashing your living room. Modify the game and play sock wars instead. Ball up about twenty-five old socks. You now have softer and safer objects for you and your children to play with indoors. Think small, and remember the old adage that less is more. Charlie and I always joke that we once had to do one of our trainings in a stairwell because that was the only place available. This was a much smaller space than we had anticipated, but we were still able to do our whole six-hour training. We used creative-play dynamics to modify the activities to fit the limited space. Though at times it felt a bit cramped, joy was still experienced by all present.

Birthday parties don't have to be expensive. We've played just about every one of these games at birthday gatherings and laughed until our sides ached. Your home or the local park are perfect places to play. You can plan either inside or outside activities and not have to worry about the weather. Maybe start with something like the Walkman of the '50s until everyone arrives, then progress to who's in charge? Younger children will play ghost and safety haven until they burn off some energy, and then you can play cooperative musical chairs and Simon says times two. (Imagine two independent and simultaneous Simon-says games; players who do something without Simon's permission are not kicked out of the game but merely join the other group.) Older kids like giants, elves, and wizards, triad, and strategy tag. If it's hot outside, you'll probably want to play sponge wars, but be sure to set some limits, such as not dumping buckets of water on any of the players. Since balloons are almost always present, you will probably want to play balloon soccer. To cut down on the cost of balloons, or if you are playing with young children who might be frightened by the sound of popping balloons, modify the game so that the goalies are instructed not to pop the balloons. Instead, goalies throw the three balloons that are always in play back into the group immediately after they catch one. At one party, there were six helium balloons, and we invented a game on the spot of racing the balloons across the ceiling by hitting them with rubber bands to make them move. Most important, adults don't have to remain spectators. Invite everyone present at the party to join in the fun. You may need to encourage parents and older guests to join more than once, but they'll always have a better time once they get involved.

The goal of teen sleep-overs does not have to be a contest of who can rent and endure the most video games and movies for the night. Probably one of the best games for teens is called I seek justice.

I SEEK JUSTICE

(Five to thirty players, a deck of cards)

How It's Played

The object of this mystery activity is for the players to discover the identity of one among them whose task is to eliminate the others. Players sit cross-legged on the floor in a circle. A deck of cards equal in number to the number of players and containing an ace of spades is required. Each player takes one card and passes the rest to the others until all cards are handed out. No one is permitted to see another's card. The person with the ace of spades is the eliminator for that round. The cards are then placed facedown in front of each player, and the players now join hands. Hands are placed behind the knees, hidden from view. Only the eliminator is allowed to initiate the elimination of others. This is accomplished by the eliminator gently squeezing the hand of the player to his right or left any number of times, up to the number of players in the game minus one (we don't want the eliminator removing himself from the game). Each player in succession squeezes the next person's hand one less time than their hand has been squeezed. For example, the eliminator squeezes the hand of the person to his right three times. That person will squeeze the hand of the person to his right two times. In turn, this person will squeeze the next person's hand once. If a player has his hand squeezed only once, he is eliminated from the game. Dramatic and humorous exits from the game are highly encouraged. Because one must always seek justice, all players become master detectives. If at any time a player, acting as a great detective, thinks he knows the identity of the eliminator, he shouts out, "I seek justice!" Before he announces who he thinks the eliminator is, he will need another person to collaborate with who will state courageously, "Me, too!" This collaboration cannot come from any eliminated players, who now watch in amusement as other players get to act out their Oscar-winning performances. If a player does get a viable collaborator and guesses the correct identity of the protagonist, the round is over, and another round may be started. However, if the guess is incorrect, both the guesser and his or her collaborator become eliminated. This game becomes even more exciting as the eliminator quickly attempts multiple successive eliminations from both her right and her left to ward off deductive guesses from the group.

So how would you modify this game to meet the needs of your small group of only four teenagers? Using creative-play dynamics, it is simple. First off, remove the concepts of sitting in a circle and holding hands. The person who has drawn the ace of spades eliminates others by a mere sly and sneaky wink to another. Once again, dramatic exits (and who better to do them than teenagers?) are encouraged. Detectives no longer need another person to collaborate their hunch. *Voilà!* A game once needing many now needs only a few.

A group of six or more can play this game for hours. One of our favorite things to do with I seek justice is to start the game and then begin doing other things throughout the evening. The I seek justice game is now paced much slower while teens stay busy making snacks, talking, or doing another activity. It's okay to have twice as much fun. Games like spoons, ninety-nine, I doubt it, and the dice game are also perfect for this age-group.

I remember as a child driving with my father and three cousins to camp and trying to solve the logic puzzle of blue magic. It seemed like it took me forever to catch on to how the game worked, but by the time I got to camp I had the answer. Then I was ready to teach the game to everyone in my cabin and begin making new friends. Lost identity is another perfect game to play in the car on a long trip. A trip to Washington can break the monotony anytime you pass a new town or city. Guessing what Aunt Tilly Willy likes and doesn't like could make the time pass quickly for a lot of miles. Take the headphones off everyone in the car and learn to enjoy one another.

For the past twelve years our family has sought vacation destinations without televisions. We've even had the management remove a set when one was present. When you start playing just to have fun, it's amazing how many activities everyone in the family wants to play. We've done ecology scavenger hunts, played low score, and even made up our own crisscross Monopoly board, which has additional properties running through the middle of it. Ninety-nine and the dice game are traditional favorites with us.

We even planned my wife's parents' fiftieth wedding anniversary party at one of our favorite vacation locations and had all the uncles, aunts, nieces, and nephews present for four days. Initially, there was concern from some of the family about what would we all do for four days but, in reality, there wasn't a single boring moment. Simple, made-up games like hitting a volley ball to all family members standing in a circle would last forty-five minutes. Adults and teens often found themselves playing cards, charades, or puzzles until one or two in the morning. Not once did the teens or adults plan a side trip to go to a movie or video arcade. We opted not to watch TV, even though the Olympics were on. We were creating an Olympic event of our own.

This year at Thanksgiving, turn off the football games for a while and play going on a picnic or action words. After everyone has gotten a little playful, you'll be ready to play personality. A game like this on Thanksgiving will remind everyone in your family that holidays are for sharing what we appreciate in one another.

Families have a lot more to offer one another than just to sit together and be entertained by others.

When playing with your smaller family unit, remember it is not the games you play that are important. Instead, focus on how you play the games. This is why the philosophy and rules are so very important. They are so important that they must extend even beyond game activities. The kids are fighting over which channel to watch on television? Well, it sounds like they are not having fun. It's time to use rule number two. Inform the kids that they must leave the television room to settle their disagreement peacefully. And in the meantime, switch the channel to the show that *you* want to watch.

For family units, think smaller, reduce the boundaries, and slow the game down. Look at the essence of the game and trim. For instance, at the heart of giants, elves, and wizards is the simple concept of the children's game rock, paper, and scissors: Each element has both a greater and a lesser value than the others. With this as your focus, you won't need many participants or even running to play this game. You could do it with two players standing in place. On the count of three, one player shows the other which character they chose. Remember, giants beat elves, elves beat wizards, and wizards beat giants. If you are the player who has a higher value than the other, you get to start the next countdown. And who says it has to be giants, elves, and wizards? It could be elephants, otters, and vacuum cleaners. Great fun occurs as you personalize your own family version.

Play in the Neighborhood

Bring play to your neighborhood. Being with your children and their friends is an issue of both quality and *quantity* time. Kids don't have to be in leagues to play sports. We adults have made life far too complicated for us and our children. What works is just to be with them after work and on weekends. It often takes less time commitment and management to join your children's lives this way than to have them on a team. In fact, it's really quite relaxing when you're not trying to win anything, just having fun with people you love.

When my son started third grade and joined his first sports league, I realized that he had joined because everyone else had. If you weren't on the team, you were basically alone in the neighborhood. The teams were fun but a lot of work and commitment from parents for twelve to sixteen weeks.

My solution was to start the Sunday free-play games. My modeling for this came from my father and all the other fathers in my neighborhood as a child. At least five nights of every week during summer vacation, we kids played kick ball in the street. There were always at least two fathers who supervised the games, and sometimes as many as six. The other parents pulled up chairs and chatted with each other on the sidelines. No parents screamed at us to do better or became obnoxious, red-faced, obscenity-yelling monsters because the umpire made a call against their kid. The parents either played with us or happily watched us have a good time being kids. No pressure. Wow! There's an idea for how to learn how to play.

On my very first week at the park with my son and about eight of his friends, I met another father playing with his kids. I asked Steve if he wanted to join and immediately made a good friend. Between the two of us we played at the park on Sundays probably forty weeks a year for the next four years. At times as many as twenty-four kids showed up, but often there were a dozen or so. We mostly played traditional games. However, they were all modified with the *Learning to Play, Playing to Learn* philosophy. Your team's score didn't count in flag football until everyone caught a pass. Everyone had to have a turn as quarterback. In basketball, the fathers could only block three kids' shots in a game. Five-year-olds played with twelve-year-olds, big with small, fast with slow. It was grex!

When older kids tried to bring a mean aggressiveness to the

games, the fathers present established that such behavior was not acceptable. Everyone was welcome to play with us, but our games were just for fun without hurting anyone. Many of these once-aggressive kids stayed and only a few chose to leave.

For those two hours every Sunday, the park and the games were ours. The kids were safe; free from neighborhood bullies or undesirable criminal pressures and supervised by playful adults. No one had to pay any enrollment fees, offer birth certificates, buy special uniforms, sell candy bars, or make banners in order to play. When your family had other plans for the day, you could miss a Sunday without any feelings that you were letting the team down. Heck, we picked different teams every thirty minutes. Everyone played with everyone as friends. Trophies were represented by smiles.

As our kids grew up, they joined the adults playing basketball. For years I continued to play twice a week with Forrest, his friends, other fathers, and their kids. Even now, they still play every week. As always, there is a special "gift of the game." In this case, it became the tradition of celebrating one another's birthdays. It is absolutely wonderful to see six semi-macho men and six testosterone-filled teen boys finish their basketball game and sit down to open silly cards, blow out candles, and stuff their face with birthday cake.

Playful Adults

Don't be afraid to have fun! One of our favorite comments at the end of a training is when someone states, "I can't wait to have a party and do this with my friends." The benefits from play occur for all ages. Adult play groups are the best. Over the years, our friends have played all the games in this book and the ones that will be in our next book. It's easier to play sit-down games with adults, but the physical activities often offer the most enjoyment when they are played compassionately.

For years now, I and my adult friends have been playing kick the can. Yep, the very same game we played as kids but now played by forty-year-olds. It's better as an adult, because now when you run off to hide in the bushes you can make out with your wife before you try to kick the can. This is a truly major improvement that I didn't even think of when I was ten. Our kick-the-can games got so popular that we soon had to keep them a secret because we only wanted ten players. One night, more than twenty people showed up all dressed in their darkest camouflage clothes. Of course, we modified the rules so that no one could be it for more than fifteen minutes and you could only be it once a night. Adults are very creative with their strategies in play. One player got a woman walking her baby in a big baby buggy to stroll toward the can while she crouched behind the buggy. She snuck right up on the can and kicked it before she was ever seen by the person who was it. One of the funniest scenes I can remember occurred when one of our friends who was very eight months' pregnant tried to outsprint a young teen who was trying to kick the can. It truly put in perspective the concept of competing against time, space, and gravity. FYI, she got to the can first!

We encourage you to play as adults. It's worth taking the healthy risk to lead these activities with your friends. If you aren't ready to be the leader, we encourage you to be an active follower of the natural playmaster in your group. Be supportive and compassionate with your friends, for many adults, just like children, need to learn how to play.

Playing with Scouts and Other Children's Groups

Learning to Play activities, rules, and philosophies are perfect for Girl Scouts, Boy Scouts, Campfire Girls, 4-H clubs, and other youth groups. The games will help teach and reinforce the values that your organization represents. Besides, after sitting all day in school, the kids are ready for some good, clean, wholesome action.

At a recent training one of the parents was so excited with triple tag and endangered species that she couldn't wait to try them with her scout troop that evening. She got the kids together and immediately started playing. To her absolute disappointment, the outcome of their games were horrible. The kids played just as poorly as they always had. They were mean and rough, and they argued constantly for twenty minutes until she stopped the games. At that point, she smartly went back to the beginning of our program. She had the kids sit down and make the posters to answer the two key questions and explained the two essential rules. Afterward, they went back and played the same games but now had fun. The children ran, laughed, and cared for each other.

As a scout leader, try figuring out which merit badges can be earned by playing in a healthy manner. Maybe a new merit badge will need to be created. If your scout group is located at a school or a church, be sure to do the eco-walk activity to clean up the play area, and praise the kids for this good-citizenship act. Delegate responsibility to your scouts by having two of them plan the game period for next week. This is great for promoting leadership skills. Make sure they know what equipment they will need to have, and let them read this book for ideas. If they forget to plan something, you may want to allow this situation, when appropriate, to be a lesson learned by not having the game period. They won't forget more than once. Being the scout leader doesn't mean you have to do all the work. In fact, it's more effective when you share these suitable tasks with your kids.

Play with Church and Synagogue Groups

Church is fun.

We did a training four years ago at a church for their middle-school-age children. Ever since, their Tuesday-night group has made play a part of their activity agenda. Some of the kids who first started with us now go back to carry on the tradition by teaching the games and playing with the new kids. What a perfect way to have the young people in your church live out the values your church group represents.

Teen retreats are a regular part of many synagogues and churches. The objective of most church retreats is to teach younger members of the congregation the beliefs of their faith. Without a doubt, you will find dozens of the games in this book perfect for your teen or children's retreat. Often retreats will have a specific theme for the weekend. Use your creative-play dynamics to change the names of the games in this book so that the play activity reflects the goals you are trying to achieve. A trip to Washington could easily become a trip to Jerusalem. Safety haven might be called love thy neighbor. Generally, when games are played with compassion for all people, every activity in this book will lend itself to achieving your positive goals. Healthy teamwork and cooperation are achieved by playing three-ball soccer or over, under, and around kick ball. Endangered species and vennis are perfect fun breaks for teens and can easily be added to a day-long agenda. In the evening, when you are trying to set a quieter tone, your group will attain maximum benefit from such trust activities as action/reaction, copy machine, and personality. Your teens will probably want to play personality all night long if they're anything like the teens we've played with. Always remember to save time at the end of your game period to discuss the positive. These discussions will reinforce everything that you are hoping to achieve on your retreat.

Another wonderful thing that your church or synagogue teen group can do is to plan the activities for the annual family picnic. This is the perfect place for teens to make responsible contributions to their church community. When planning several hours of play, be sure to have a balance of active and quiet activities.

Begin by having teens practice out loud, explaining the rules and the expectations of how the games are to be played. Have the teens practice playing the games themselves so they know what to expect. (A gentle reminder: Often teenagers are very self-conscious and reluctant to do silly things like playing games. Teens have their sense of cool to maintain. Additionally, they've already watched too many adults sit and become spectators in life and naturally have begun to emulate them. By giving your teen group the responsibility of leading the games, you are adding a new factor to the equation for breaking down their self-conscious barriers. Now, not only is there a specific reason to do the games, but they quickly discover that they are also having a grex time. Once this barrier is broken, it becomes a safe, acceptable norm of your teen group to play. They will become more open to other healthy risks and have greater fun with each other.)

Games are also perfect for your church singles groups. Nothing mixes people up faster than games that allow everyone to relax and meet each other without any unnecessary expectations. Start off with light, breezy games like oh, Fido or change are you a PeaceBuilder? to do you like fun dates? ("Yes, and I like fun dates that ______.") After a while, a game of empathy would be funny and enjoyable. If you start to play kick the can, we'll know you've read the other parts of our book.

Playing at Work

"Our company makes widgets. I don't pay people to play games and have fun. I pay them to do their job!" This is the way many employers feel about work. This statement is most often made by the highly valued, extremely productive executive who conducts some of the company's most important business on the golf course or at the racket club. It's time to stop the double standard of who can have fun while doing work. If you want a big boost in company morale, let play be a positively sanctioned part of your employees' workday.

Of course, we're not advocating that you close down the office and let everyone play golf for four hours every Thursday. That's not where the majority of employees can work or play to get their job done. What we are advocating is that the same dynamics that help the executive land big deals at the golf course (being playful, relaxed, open, happy, and creative and having enjoyable camaraderie with others) are the same essential needs of every worker, every day, in every company.

In order to bring play into the workplace, management must wholeheartedly endorse it. Employees cannot sense any doubt that appropriate playfulness will be viewed as poor work performance. It's best when the boss models playful activities or is present for them. At one company we worked at, our boss encouraged us to play every Friday afternoon. The last four work hours of the week were always the most stressful and the busiest, yet we were always encouraged to take our 2:45 P.M. break together and do something fun. We did such things as seeing who could slide in their socks the farthest on the gleaming solid oak floor in the board room. (Women wearing nylons really slid well.) We held a staple-removing contest to see who could collect the most staples out of ten on the upper side of their staple remover. (The secretarial staff was by far the best at this, but everyone, including the boss, tried.) Sometimes we even had prizes. The most popular prize at our organization was first-in-line privileges at the copy machine anytime on Monday. These fun breaks essentially renewed our energy, made us relaxed, and kept us in contact with different people from different departments. Then we went back to our office feeling renewed and worked real hard.

At your business, some afternoon, clear out a space and put some chairs in a circle and play oh, Fido with your employees. If a customer walks in, add a chair for him. We know of one boss who had so much fun with this game that he periodically yells, "Oh, Fido!" during meetings when people are getting that blank, glazed-over look. This is a signal for everyone to get up and move to another chair. Sometimes he does it two or three times in a row. It doesn't take much time, but it gets people attentive while having some fun.

One manager in a technology department picked up half a dozen noise-making ray guns and gave them to everyone in the office. That afternoon, and on other spontaneous occasions, the employees spent odd moments sneaking up and blasting each other. Simple, quick, ongoing, and revitalizing.

As the boss, you can easily bring fifty balloons to work and play balloon soccer. We know this activity works well even in very large groups. One time we played it with 220 members of U.S. West Communications' Presidents Club, and they all loved it.

Your goal is not to turn employees into overboard pranksters but to revitalize morale and increase productivity. Have a short staff meeting to outline some goals for fun in the workplace. Obviously, squirt guns in an expensive technology department could cause a lot of expensive damage. Noise-making rays guns do no harm. Discuss among your staff the idea of people being the most important part of the company, and explain that games that honor everyone will be encouraged.

Encourage your employees to play games during their lunch break or give fifteen to twenty minutes of extra time on Monday, Wednesday, and Friday for them to join in company games. Delegate a "spirit-master" to create no-cost special events each month, and be sure the boss shows up and joins in when possible. Inexpensive equipment can allow you to play vennis-style volleyball. It's a great company game because it is so inclusive. Forget score keeping, or keep only the accumulated total of successful volleys without an error. Post the accumulated score and try to beat it the next time you play.

Remember, you are not trying to determine whether accounting has a better team than sales. What you want is for sales, janitorial, production, secretarial, accounting, data processing, and management to all mix together and get to know each other as full human beings. The benefits of playing at the office are identical to those of doing business at the golf club. Employees benefit by having a shared goal of making their company and their lives successful.

Play is productive and meaningful, and it will enhance cooperation and loyalty among coworkers.

Company picnics are the perfect place to play totally it; giants, elves, and wizards; who's in charge; rattlesnake tag; and maybe even sponge wars. There are dozens of activities in this book that are perfect for these events. What could be better than having the family and friends of your employees share the positive joy of having fun together. Feeling good about where you work and how the company treats your family is not derived from the dollars-and-cents columns on a pay check, but those feelings can make a difference in how many dollars your company ultimately generates.

It is desirable to have employees go home to spouses and friends and tell them, "You won't guess what crazy, fun thing we did at work today. Our boss got us all together with three paper wads, a buzzing pager, and an empty coffee cup [using creative-play dynamics to spontaneously adapt cosmic motions to the workplace], and we had to pass them around in different ways. It was so wild, and we laughed so hard. I'm not sure I can explain it, but it was fun. It made my time at work more enjoyable and fruitful." The alternative is, "Finally, the weekend. I'm so tired of this job. I've got a stack of work I'll never finish. It just goes on and on." Which kind of thoughts do you think will create the happier and more productive worker?

Company teams can be wonderful, but they are not what we advocate as a means to bring play to the workplace. Sometimes company teams cause as many internal morale difficulties as they were intended to help.

What we're encouraging managers and employees to do is to choose the second strongest motivator in forging cooperation: fun. Fun forges cooperation quicker than any other human dynamic other than a catastrophe. Gosh, let's see here. Our organization can choose to attempt productivity through managing frequent crises or by having fun at work. Well, duh, which one would you like your company to choose?

Some wise men once said, "If you can't play together, how can you possibly work together?" Oh, that was us. In his book *This Job Should Be Fun,* Bob Basso, Ph.D., states that the values found in healthy play—fun, open communication, teamwork, and innovation—are the same ones found in the most productive companies on our planet. We hope you are ready to bring play into the workplace. If you are ready but feel you'd like some expert help getting started, give us a call. After all, our whole business is about playing while you work.

Play Belongs Everywhere

If you've read everything in this book to this point, we can tell we're probably preaching to the choir. You clearly understand how play can make you feel. You know how it can teach valuable lessons, bring people closer together, make us laugh, compete, cooperate, allow us to care, be silly and free. We at Creative Spirit hope you will share what you've learned about how to play with the other people who are important in your lives.

References and Readings

Acton, Heather M., and Lynne Zarbatany. "Interaction and performance within cooperative groups: Effects on nonhandicapped students' attitudes toward their mildly mentally retarded peers." *American Journal on Mental Retardation*, 93, 16–23 (1988).

Bay-Hinitz, April K., Robert F. Peterson, and H. Robert Quilitch. "Cooperative games: A way to modify aggressive and cooperative behaviors in young children." *Journal of Applied Behavior Analysis*, 27, 435–446 (1994).

Blank, M., and B.R. McCandless. "A methodology for fostering abstract thinking in deprived children." Ontario Institute for Studies in Education, Monograph, 9, 1–25 (1970).

Embry, D.D., D.J. Flannery, A.T. Vazsonyi, K. Powell, and H. Atha. "PeaceBuilders: A theoretically driven, school-based model for early violence prevention." *American Journal of Preventive Medicine*, 12, 91–100 (1996).

Fluegelman, Andrew. *New Games*. New York: Bantam Doubleday Dell Publishing Group, Inc., 1976.

———. *More New Games*. New York: Bantam Doubleday Dell Publishing Group, Inc., 1981.

Loomans, Diane, and Karen Kolberg. *The Laughing Classroom.* Tiburon, Calif: H. J. Kramer, Inc., 1993.

Murphy, H.A., J.M. Hutchinson, and J.S. Bailey. "Behavioral school psychology goes outdoors: The effects of organized games on playground aggression." *Journal of Applied Behavior Analysis,* 16, 29–35 (1983).

Orlick, Terry. *The 1st & 2nd Cooperative Sports and Games Book.* New York: Random House Inc., 1982. (excellent for younger children)

Pellegrini, A.D. "Elementary-school children's rough-and-tumble play and social competence." *Developmental Psychology,* 24, 802–806 (1988).

Rogers, M. "Cooperative games as an intervention to promote cross-racial acceptance." *American Educational Research Journal,* 18, 513–16 (1981).

Sapp, M. "Irrational beliefs that can lead to academic failure for African American middle school students who are academically at-risk." *Journal of Rational-Emotive & Cognitive Behavior Therapy,* 14, 123–134 (1996).

Thomas, Jerry R., and Amelia M. Lee, Lea McGee, and Stephen Silverman. "Effects of individual and group contingencies on disruptive playground behavior." *Journal of Research & Development in Education,* 20, 66–76 (1987).

Walker, H.M., G. Colvin, and E. Ramsey. *Anti-social behavior in schools: Strategies and best practices.* Pacific Grove, Calif: Brooks/Cole, 1995.

Weinstein, Matt, and Joel Goodman. *Playfair.* San Luis Obispo, Calif: Impact Publishers, 1980.

White, A.G., and J.S. Bailey. "Reducing disruptive behaviors of elementary special education students with sit and watch." *Journal of Applied Behavior Analysis,* 23, 353–60 (1990).

Index

1. Games by Names

2. Games by Behaviors You Want to Manage or Promote

Remember that every game opens itself to a variety of behaviors and skills that it can address. The following games are suggestions based on years of experiencing repetitive benefits from their use. However, we encourage you to use an open mind and look towards other games to achieve results that you desire.

Abstract Thinking

Appropriate Touching

Complimenting Others

Communication

Conflict Resolution

Cooperation

Decreasing Figidity Behaviors

Empathy

Helping Others

Holding Hands

Imagination

Improving Math Skills

Including Everybody

Learning Names

Safety

Self-Control

Standing in Line

Teamwork

Venting Aggression

3. Games by Age-Groups

Remember that every game opens itself to a variety of age-groups by utilizing creative-play dynamics. For instance, we know of a kindergarten teacher who routinely plays cosmic motions, a game often played by teens, with his four- and five-year-olds. And even though the game of personality requires abstract thought, we know of a second-grade teacher whose children adore playing this game. In a reverse manner, if you don't tell your fifth graders that broken wheel is really just advanced duck, duck, goose, they will play this activity with as much youthful abandon as do first graders. Charlie and I fondly remember having a psychiatric unit full of adolescent boys, all diagnosed as having conduct disorders, willingly playing broken wheel. We smartly never told them they were just playing advanced duck, duck, goose. The lesson here is to remain open and you will find that a great majority of these games transcend age barriers.

P = primary (grades K–2); I = intermediate (grades 2–6); T = teens; A = adults. A question mark means the appropriateness of this activity depends on your assessment of your particular groups abilities.